Welcome to Rome

David and Marie-Claire Willey

Collins
Glasgow and London

Cover photographs
Van Phillips
(top; Trinità dei Monti and Spanish Steps, Castel S. Angelo
centre, Dome of St Peter's Basilica from Vatican Gardens
bottom; Colosseum, Arch of Constantine)

Photographs
All photographs, Van Phillips
except pp 80–1, ZEFA
and p. 121, Italian State Tourist Office

Illustrations
pp. 4–9 Peter Joyce

Maps
pp. 37–53 adapted by kind permission of Hallwag
from their city map series
pp. 68–75 M. and R. Piggott

First published 1981
Copyright © William Collins Sons and Company Limited
Published by William Collins Sons and Company Limited
Printed in Great Britain
ISBN 0 00 447314 0

CONTENTS

Every effort has been made to give you an up-to-date text but changes are constantly occurring and we will be grateful for any information about changes you may notice while travelling.

For over two thousand years Rome has exercised an important and sometimes decisive influence over the history of western civilization. Rome's fortunes, and its population, have fluctuated wildly; from being the cosmopolitan hub of one of the most powerful military empires of the ancient world, Rome dwindled to little more than an overgrown village of a few thousand inhabitants during the Middle Ages, to become again a new world centre of religion and the arts under the Popes of the Renaissance, and finally capital of the modern Italian state since 1870.

The continuity of two millenia of urban living is written into the palaces, churches, ruins, fountains, even the street names of Rome. The visitor has only to look at a building, to read an inscription, in order to be projected back through the centuries. A walk in Rome is a walk through time. Romans have experienced practically every form of good and bad government and law-making known to mankind. They take their city's long and distinguished history and culture very much for granted, and you must forgive them if they regard the earnest sightseer more as someone to be exploited or even, alas, to be robbed, rather than someone who has come to pay tribute at the fountain-head of western Christendom.

Take the trouble, however, to carry out certain basic security precautions, such as never leaving your luggage unguarded, or carrying large sums of cash around with you, arm yourself with a few words of Italian, and you will find that the modern Romans can also be charming, helpful and understanding of the poor foreigner who comes to get acquainted with their venerable city.

Although Rome is the seat of government in Italy and the headquarters of the Roman Catholic Church, it is not one of the humming capital cities of Europe. Milan is Italy's economic and financial centre. Rome is a city of priests, pilgrims and bureaucrats – it has practically no industry except for the tourist trade. The rapid growth of mass tourism has caused transit problems inside the city wall, a relatively small area, which encompasses only four per cent of modern metropolitan Rome's 600 square miles. Traffic problems are nothing new, however. In 45 BC Julius Caesar issued an edict banning wheeled traffic from the city centre during daylight hours. The result was that Romans' sleep was disturbed at night by the sound of cartwheels on the cobbled streets. 'Where can you find lodgings that give you the chance to get a night's rest?' a celebrated Latin writer asked, a question that must have been repeated by millions of modern tourists.

Rome enjoys a continental climate tempered by its nearness to the sea and it southern latitude. Average daytime temperatures range from 7°C in January to 25°C in July. Winters are short but can be cold. Snow is very rare indeed. The best months for a visit are May, June, September and October. It used to be fashionable for foreigners to winter in Rome during the 18th and 19th centuries, but now most tourists come in summer. The absence of many Romans during the normally hot months of July and August means that it is easier to circulate in the city in high

summer, although you may find many shops and restaurants closed in August.

Legend relates that the city was founded on 21 April 753 BC by King Romulus. The God of War, Mars had fathered twin sons destined to be sacrificed by drowning in the river Tiber. But the infant boys were saved when a shepherd, Faustulus, found them and took them home to his wife, who brought them up. The boys had been suckled and protected by an unusual foster-mother – a she-wolf – after being left for dead in the swamps near the river. They were given the names Romulus and Remus, and when they came of age, traced the future city walls with a sacred plough. Romulus killed Remus after a dispute over who should give his name to the city. Rome's birthday is still celebrated every year on 21 April and all dates in ancient times were calculated from the year in which Romulus was believed to have named the city. The year was followed not by the letters BC or AD as in our reckoning, but by the initials a.u.c.; *ab urbe condita*, from the foundation of the city.

Latest archaeological research suggests that the foundation of Rome ought to be dated at least two centuries earlier than the traditional date. It is extremely difficult to make the archaeological and the historical record mesh. All that one can say for certain is that Rome quickly became pre-eminent among a group of Iron Age settlements in Lazio (Latium). and that there was a bitter power struggle with the Etruscan city states to the north during the 5th century BC which ended in ultimate victory for Rome over a civilization which was certainly cultu-

rally more advanced. The Latin language (using Etruscan symbols for 21 out of its 23 letters of the alphabet) came into general use during this time.

An invasion by Gallic armies from the north in 390 BC left the city in ruins and temporarily checked the spread of Roman power. But soon Rome expanded its control over the whole Italian peninsula. By 270 BC the Greek colonies of southern Italy were under Roman control. Culturally, this military absorbtion of Magna Graecia had a major influence on the subsequent development of Roman taste in art, literature and architecture. Two dramatic wars with Carthage lasted for over 50 years, during which the brilliant Carthaginian General Hannibal attacked from the north, crossing the Alps and inflicting a serious military defeat on Rome's armies at Lake Trasimene in 217 BC. After finally defeating Hannibal and making further conquests in Spain and in the eastern Mediterranean, Rome became the undisputed leader of the Mediterranean world. The streets of the city were now paved for the first time, stone bridges were thrown across the Tiber, aqueducts were built to provide water for a teeming city that already counted its inhabitants in hundreds of thousands. Heavy migration and the growth of a large slave population created slums and serious problems of urban living. There was neither a police force nor a fire brigade to deal with frequent outbreaks of fire.

The Emperor Augustus (27 BC–AD 14) was the first ruler of Rome to transform the city into a great imperial capital worthy of the name. His boast

that he found Rome brick and left it marble was not exaggerated. Public buildings of huge and noble proportions, baths, temples and theatres mushroomed during his reign and he set up the first regular police and fire fighting services. Claudius (AD 41–54) built the port of Ostia at the mouth of the Tiber to improve direct grain shipments to feed the growing population. Nero (AD 54–68) rebuilt a large area of the city devastated by the great fire of AD 64 as well a creating his fabled pleasure palace, the Golden House. Trajan (AD 98–117) built a great forum, a huge complex with shops, public baths, libraries and meeting halls, a forerunner of the modern convention centre. Two of the major monuments of the Emperor Hadrian (AD 117–138) survive in modern Rome, the domed Pantheon and the Emperor's Mausoleum, now known as the Castel Sant'Angelo.

Huge numbers of slaves, the victims of military conquest, swelled the population to over a million. New multi-storey apartment buildings, the first in history, tended to make living conditions for most city dwellers overcrowded and shoddy. Side by side with the splendid marble palaces were slums where the refinements of Rome's extraordinarily inventive technology; running water, heated baths and piped sewage disposal, were unknown.

As the first Christians gathered to worship in the catacombs and other secret meeting places, the seeds of Imperial decay and decline were already being sown. Plague and fire decimated the population. Two thousand corpses a day were being carted off for burial during a bad plague in the reign of Marcus Aurelius. By the end of the 3rd century AD the Emperor Aurelian was forced to build a huge defensive wall eleven miles long around the city (much of it still survives) to repel the increasing number of attacks by barbarian invaders. Rome was on the defensive for the first time in centuries. Malaria spread over the surrounding countryside.

The centre of Empire shifted eastwards with the founding of Constantinople, the 'New Rome', by Constantine (AD 306–337), the first Christian Emperor. Although he restored many of the buildings of Imperial times, the decline of the city was hastened by being sacked several times; in AD 410 the Visigoths of Alaric's army burnt and pillaged the city for three days, in AD 455 the Vandals spent fourteen days looting and destroying the riches of Rome. But perhaps the greatest damage of all was caused by the Romans themselves. For many generations it became the custom to strip the monuments and great public buildings of their marbles and to quarry building materials from the remains of the greatest architectural achievements of the ancient world. By the middle of the 6th century AD, Rome had become a mere appendage of the Byzantine Empire, whose chief city in Italy was Ravenna, on the Adriatic coast.

Civil authority passed into the hands of the Church, and the Bishops of Rome, perforce, temporal rulers. The Papacy turned for military protection to the Franks and the history

of Rome took a significant new turn with the coronation of Charlemagne as Holy Roman Emperor by Pope Leo III in 800. The division of spiritual and temporal power was to be bitterly disputed for centuries. After the Muslims plundered St Peter's in 846, Pope Leo IV built a defensive wall around the Vatican suburb that became known as the Leonine city. For the next 200 years, control of the Papacy and of the city was disputed between various noble Roman families, with occasional intervention from German Emperors. Another major sack of the city took place in 1084 when the Normans under Robert Guiscard pillaged and destroyed many buildings.

The Commune of Rome was first established after a revolution against Papal authority in 1144, and in 1188 the civil government of the city was formally recognized by the reigning Pope. But factional and territorial disputes between Rome's leading Papal families, the Orsini, the Colonna and the Annibaldi, led to a decline in law and order and in wealth. In 1309 the Popes moved out of Rome to Avignon in France where they remained until 1377. The plague called the Black Death reduced the population to a few thousand wretched inhabitants and Rome reached its nadir around 1400 when according to contemporary chroniclers wolves roamed at night in the vicinity of St Peter's. The prestigious Capitoline Hill became known as Monte Caprino (Goat Hill) while the Forum, the former city centre, was used for pasture and was known henceforth as Campo Vaccino (Cow Field).

From the beginning of the 15th century, the Popes took over local government and finance and began to embellish the city with fine new edifices. But at the same time they authorized the destruction of many of the remaining buildings of antiquity whose valuable marbles were sometimes reused but more often ended up in lime kilns. However, the Popes of the Renaissance superimposed a new city of unparalleled splendour upon the remains of the past. They attracted artists, architects and scholars from many parts of Italy and commissioned what turned out to be some of the supreme achievements of European art, among them Michelangelo's design for the new St Peter's and his decoration of the Sistine Chapel. Basilicas and churches were rebuilt and extended. New conventual buildings, patrician palaces and streets replaced the crumbling and haphazardly built medieval city.

Another sack, in 1527, by the armies of the Holy Roman Emperor Charles V, brought this period of Renaissance development to a temporary halt. But the Popes of the Counter-reformation soon began building again. The new St Peter's replaced the basilica commemorating the first apostle which had endured since the time of Constantine. Pope Sixtus V (1585–90) was a great and inspired town planner. He cut new thoroughfares through Rome, laid out piazze, raised fallen obelisks, rebuilt the Lateran and Vatican Palaces. The great 17th-century architect and sculptor Gian Lorenzo Bernini adorned the city with numerous buildings and works of art.

The population of Rome began to rise again, reaching 165,000 by the time Napoleon's armies occupied the city in 1798; the Pope was deported to France in order to take part in the coronation ceremony of the new Emperor in Notre Dame in Paris. In 1809 Rome and the Papal States were formally annexed into the French Empire while Napoleon was sufficiently mindful of Rome's past glories to name his infant son 'King of Rome'. After Napoleon's defeat and exile, the old order was re-established and for several decades the Papacy exercised a harsh rule in its attempts to stave off constitutional reform. Pope Pius IX granted the city a constitution in 1848 but after the revolution of 1848–9 called in the French again to restore his temporal power.

Rome was excluded from the new united Kingdom of Italy proclaimed in 1861, and another ten years passed before Italian troops under the command of Giuseppe Garibaldi breached the city walls in 1870 to complete the unification of Italy. Rome was officially proclaimed capital in 1871. The Pope declined to come to terms with the new secular government choosing to remain what he termed 'the prisoner of the Vatican'. It was not until the Fascist dictator Benito Mussolini signed the Lateran Pacts in 1929 that the Pope's sovereignty over Vatican City was formally recognized. Meanwhile, Rome's population had been growing rapidly, passing the half million mark before the First World War and doubling again to more than a million during the first years of the Fascist regime by the late 1920s. Huge new suburbs grew up around the ancient city. Mussolini ordered the carrying out of widespread archaeological excavations in the city centre, levelling whole medieval quarters to create the Via della Conciliazione, leading to the Vatican, and his own Triumphal Way, the Via dei Fori Imperiali.

After the collapse of the Fascist government in 1943 during the Second World War, Rome was under brief German occupation until the liberation by Allied armies in June 1944. Apart from the bombing of S. Lorenzo fuori le Mura, the city escaped almost intact from the war. With a population now exceeding three million, the main threat to Rome today has become uncontrolled building speculation. Many ancient *palazzi* have been gutted inside to transform them into multi-apartment buildings, but on the whole, the external aspect of the honey-coloured city centre within the walls has been preserved more successfully than the centres of most other European capitals. If you climb up on to the Gianicolo at sunset and look out over the domes and the campaniles, the umbrella pines of the Villa Medici, with the Alban hills rising behind in the background, you will still be rewarded with one of the most sublime skylines in the world. Here, at your feet, lies the city to which all roads once led.

It is often difficult for the non-specialist to make sense out of Rome's history without some ready reference to the most important Emperors and Popes who left their imprint upon the city. The following list is not exhaustive, but indicates names in both Italian and English, with dates.

Emperors

Augusto	(Augustus)	27 BC –	AD	14
Tiberio	(Tiberius)	AD 14 –		37
Caligula	(Caligula)	AD 37 –		41
Nerone	(Nero)	AD 54 –		68
Vespasiano	(Vespasian)	AD 69 –		79
Tito	(Titus)	AD 79 –		81
Domiziano	(Domitian)	AD 81 –		96
Nerva	(Nerva)	AD 96 –		98
Traiano	(Trajan)	AD 98 –		117
Adriano	(Hadrian)	AD 117 –		138
Marco Aurelio	(Marcus Aurelius)	AD 161 –		180
Settimio Severo	(Septimius Severus)	AD 193 –		211
Caracalla	(Caracalla)	AD 211 –		217
Costantino	(Constantine)	AD 306 –		337

Popes

(The number preceding the name indicates order of succession since St Peter)

1	S. Pietro	(St Peter) martyred in Rome	AD 64 or 67
64	S. Gregorio I	(St Gregory the Great) Roman	590–604
170	Adriano IV	(Adrian IV) Nicholas Breakspear, the only English Pope	1154–1159
211	Pio II	(Pius II) Enea Silvio Piccolomini	1458–1464
215	Alessandro VI	(Alexander VI) Rodrigo Borgia	1492–1503
217	Giulio II	(Julius II) Giuliano della Rovere	1503–1513
218	Leone X	(Leo X) Giovanni de' Medici	1513–1521
219	Adriano VI	(Adrian VI) Adrian Florenz from Utrecht, last non-Italian Pope until election of John Paul II	1522–1523
232	Clemente VIII	(Clement VIII) Ippolito Aldobrandini	1592–1605
234	Paolo V	(Paul V) Camillo Borghese	1605–1621
236	Urbano VIII	(Urban VIII) Maffeo Barberini	1623–1644
237	Innocenzo X	(Innocent X) Giovanni Battista Pamphilj	1644–1655
238	Alessandro VII	(Alexander VII) Fabio Chigi	1655–1667
256	Pio IX	(Pius IX) Giovanni Maria Mastai-Ferretti	1846–1878
260	Pio XI	(Pius XI) Achille Ratti	1922–1939
261	Pio XII	(Pius XII) Eugenio Pacelli	1939–1958
262	Giovanni XXIII	(John XXIII) Angelo Roncalli	1958–1963
263	Paolo VI	(Paul VI) Giovanni Battista Montini	1963–1978
264	Giovanni Paolo I	(John Paul I) Albino Luciani	1978
265	Giovanni Paolo II	(John Paul II) Karol Wojtyla	1978

PAPERWORK

Passports All visitors to Italy need a valid passport and tourists are entitled to stay up to three months without any formality other than registration with the police within three days of arrival (which will normally be done automatically by your hotel or *pensione*). British, American and Canadian citizens are exempted from visa requirements and need no special health or vaccination certificates. If, however, you come to Italy for work or study you will need a *permesso di soggiorno* (residence permit) for which you must apply at the Ufficio Stranieri (Aliens' Office) at the Questura in the Via Genova (at the back of the Via Nazionale). If you need more detailed advice on residence qualifications apply to your local Italian consulate before travelling to Rome. UK visitors to Rome can travel on a *British Visitors Passport* valid for one year.

Insurance UK visitors should obtain from their doctor before leaving a copy of Form E 111 entitling them to free medical treatment in Italy, under reciprocal arrangements between the two governments. No such facility exists for American or Canadian citizens, who should check with their local health insurance company to ascertain what cover they may be entitled to under any private health policies held.

Given the generally unsatisfactory working of the Italian National Health Service, you would be well advised to take out additional private insurance against illness, accident or loss of property. Details from your local travel agent at home.

Even if you have failed to take out any special insurance and you meet with a sudden accident or illness during your stay in Rome, you will be given any necessary urgent medical treatment without payment in any Italian state hospital. The costs will be debited to you when you return home, and if for any reason you are unable to pay, they will be borne by the local health authority in Rome. If you meet with sudden illness or accident and are fit enough to travel home you would be well advised to do so immediately rather than to rely upon Italian doctors and hospitals.

Customs Visitors are entitled to bring duty-free into Italy all normal personal effects, including still and cine-cameras and film, sports equipment, and a typewriter. You can also bring in up to 400 cigarettes, one bottle of alcoholic beverage, and one small bottle of perfume.

You are *not* allowed to import drugs (imprisonment is the sanction for failure to observe Italy's severe anti-drug laws) and you need special documentation in advance to import pet animals (details from your airline or from British Railways). Firearms must be declared and deposited with customs upon arrival.

The export of original works of art is conditional upon the issue of a permit by the Ministero dei Beni Culturali, Via del Collegio Romano, Rome.

Enquiries about current customs regulations should be directed to Dogana di Roma, 8 Viale Scalo S. Lorenzo, tel 4952741, for matters relating to the import and export of goods by land or sea and to Dogana Italiana, Sezione Viaggiatori, Aeroporto di Fiumicino, tel 6011348 for visitors arriving and leaving by air.

HOW TO GET THERE

Air services

From UK: direct scheduled services from London (Heathrow) daily to Rome (Fiumicino) by British Airways and Alitalia. Journey time 2 hrs 10 mins. Excursion fares available six days minimum stay, one month maximum validity.

Charter services from London (Gatwick) and Luton to Rome (Ciampino). Also in summer only, Edinburgh and some UK provincial cities direct to Ciampino. For information enquire: Saintseal Travel, 24A Earls Court Gardens, London SW5 (Tel: 01-370 6355). St Catherine's Tours, 48, Catherine Place, London SW1 (Tel: 01-834 7651). Student Travel Bureau, 31, Buckingham Palace Rd, London SW1 (Tel: 01-828 2082).

From US: direct scheduled services from New York, and Boston by TWA, and Alitalia, Pan Am from New York. Tariffs vary according to season and type of comfort offered by up to 50 per cent. The cheapest fares are APEX and Budget which involve booking your outward and return flights at least three weeks in advance. Details from your local travel agent. Alternatively take a cheap flight to London and continue to Rome by one of the charter services mentioned above.

From Canada: direct scheduled services from Toronto and Montreal by CP Air and Alitalia. APEX and Budget fares as above. You may find it cheaper to travel via London. It will pay you to shop around for the most economical and convenient fare, particularly if you are combining Rome with other cities on your European itinerary. The main airport is Fiumicino (Leonardo Da Vinci) 30km/19mi from the city centre. Transport by bus or taxi takes 40 mins-1 hour depending upon traffic conditions. A new rail connection is planned. Charter traffic mostly arrives and departs from Ciampino (18kms/11mi). Bus or taxi journey 30 mins. Facilities for the disabled at both airports available *only upon prior advice.*

Rail

From London (Victoria) via Dover/ Boulogne/Milan to Roma (Termini), journey time 30 hours. No through service for accompanied cars, although you can travel with your car between Boulogne and Milan, which cuts a huge chunk out of the driving. Ask your local ENIT offices (see useful addresses) for details of current reductions available to foreign visitors and young people under the age of 26 on Italian railways (Ferrovie dello Stato).

Car ferry

Via Sealink Ferry or Hovercraft from Southampton/Folkestone/Dover/Ramsgate to Calais/Boulogne/Dieppe/Le Havre. The choice of overland routes to Rome is immense – but one fairly direct way is via the Mont Blanc tunnel, skirting south of Geneva, and getting straight on to the Autostrada network towards Rome. Italian motorway tolls are cheaper than the French, and the 760km/472mi from Aosta to Rome can be covered in about eight hours without racing.

No special modifications are necessary to foreign registered cars in Italy but check you have your green international insurance card in order and are carrying the correct nationality plate or sticker. A luminous red triangle for use if you happen to break down on the motorway is recommended as a useful spare. It would also be prudent to carry a small supply of basic spares (fanbelt, radiator hose, set of points) if you are driving any car except a Fiat.

Bus/coach From Victoria Coach Station, London to Milan and thence to Rome. Details from Victoria Coach Station or Student Travel Bureau, 31, Buckingham Palace Road, London SW1.

Europabus This bus service is operated by the railways of western Europe and provides swift, comfortable travel in air-conditioned buses between many towns on the continent. One can break one's journey at many places en route, but in the peak holiday season it is advisable to plan one's stops and book well in advance.

Italian towns served by Europabus include Torino, Génova, Milano, Venezia, Firenze, Ravenna, Perúgia, Roma, Nápoli, Brindisi. A great variety of tours are also available, including 5- and 7-day tours of Sicilia.

Full details from Europabus, British Railways Travel Centre, London, SW1, or Europabus (Overseas) Inc., 630 Fifth Avenue, New York 10020, USA.

Internal Communications

Trains There are four different types of trains in Italy:

Rapido; an inter-city express on which a supplement is charged.

Direttissimo; a fast train, but which stops at a few stations than does the *Rapido*; usually 1st and 2nd class booking is available.

Diretto; fairly fast, but stopping at more stations than the *Direttissimo*.

Accelerato; the slowest type of all, stopping at every station.

ACCOMMODATION

Generally speaking Rome hotels are noisy and it is necessary to get out into the suburbs to find relative peace and quiet at night. But you must weigh up in your own mind how important street and personal noise is to you as the further from the centre you stay, the more precious time you will waste shuttling back and forth for sightseeing. Here are the main hotel areas and their advantages and disadvantages.

Historic centre Noisy, can be expensive. Choose smaller hotels for charm and comfort and ask for a room on the garden or courtyard if there is one.

Parioli/Monte Mario The northern suburbs contain fashionable residential areas but they are a long way from the centre if the traffic is congested.

Aventino Quiet, and a few pleasant hotels and pensioni.

Via Veneto/Villa Borghese Expensive, but value for money in the luxury category.

Termini Avoid staying too near the Railway Station; unpleasant street scene at night, little character or charm. You might as well be staying in Milan.

Vatican/Gianicolo Many religious houses offer accommodation at reasonable rates, not limited to Roman Catholic pilgrims. Details from EPT.

Rome offers a wide range of hotels from luxury class such as the Grand, the Eden, the Excelsior and the Hassler, down to modest establishments with great charm, such as the Albergo Sole near the Pantheon and the Pensione Scalinata di Spagna at the top of the Spanish Steps. A full list of hotels and pensioni and religious establishments offering board and lodging is available from the EPT. Prices have to be displayed by law in every hotel room. If you feel you are being cheated complain to the EPT. Prices are normally higher at Easter and during the summer season. *Book in advance* if possible, as hotels are also full at certain periods during autumn and winter when various congresses and international meetings take place in Rome. The red Michelin guide, *Italy*, is usually a reliable indicator of current hotel classifications, and contains useful maps showing locations. Avoid at all costs hotel touts who accost you on arrival at Termini Railway Station. Self-catering service flatlets are available in what the Italians call 'Residences'. A list is also available from the EPT. There is a modern *Albergo Diurno* (day hotel) in the basement under Termini Railway Station where you can bathe, shave or refresh yourself while waiting for a train or after a tiring and dusty journey.

Lira banknotes are issued in the following denominations: 100,000, 50,000, 20,000, 10,000, 5000, 1000, 500. Do not be surprised if you are given different banknote issues of the same denomination – they are all legal tender. Coins are issued in values of 200 lira (gold colour), 100 lira (silver colour), 50 lira (silver colour), 10 lira (aluminium). Under current Italian exchange control regulations, visitors are bound to declare foreign currency brought into the country. Upon departure, you will only be permitted to re-exchange excess lira obtained by exchanging the currency declared upon your arrival, so keep bank exchange vouchers as evidence.

There are branches of the Banco di Santo Spirito at Fiumicino and Ciampino airports where you can exchange money outside normal banking hours, including weekends. An exchange office is also open daily 0900–2100 at the information office at Termini Railway Station. Banks are open Monday to Friday only 0830–1330 and most of the main banks are located in the Via del Corso. Be prepared for a long wait behind two different counters before you get your cash.

International credit cards, including American Express, Visa and Diners' Club are widely accepted in shops, hotels and restaurants.

Hotels usually are willing to change banknotes and travellers cheques but naturally at a lower rate than the banks. As an insurance against theft, you are recommended to bring travellers cheques rather than banknotes with you to Italy. Some stores, such as the Rinascente, in the Via del Corso give specially favourable exchange rates for foreign currency purchases.

GETTING AROUND ROME

Apart from the catacombs and one or two outlying churches, practically all the main places of interest in Rome lie within fairly easy walking distance of the city centre (Piazza Venezia). However, for those unused or unable to walk, adequate (but crowded) public transport is available and there is an efficient radio taxi service.

Metropolitana

There are two lines, *Linea A* running roughly east-west and *Linea B* north-south with an interchange at Termini Railway Station. A single fare structure operates with automatic ticket vending machines at all stations. You can also buy monthly season tickets for a modest price at metro stations and also at tobacconists shops. These can be combined with bus season tickets for the same period. First trains about 0630. Last trains about 2330. *Beware of pickpockets in crowded underground trains.*

Buses

The Rome Bus Company is called ATAC and a complete list of services is contained in the Pagine Gialle (Yellow Pages) of the Rome telephone directory (which incidentally also contains a useful street gazetteer with sectional maps of the whole city area, including the suburbs). A number of all night buses run on some routes. Bus stops are painted green and display numbers and destinations of services. Those marked *a richiesta* mean that buses stop by request only. Most bus services trail off or end about 2100. The most useful bus route for tourists is the 64 double decker service which runs from Termini Railway Station to the Vatican. But *beware pickpockets.* Most buses now have automatic fare collection. Information on bus services can be obtained from ATAC staff at Largo Argentina, Piazza Venezia, Piazza S. Silvestro, and Termini Railway Station. Season tickets valid for a whole calendar month for one or all lines can be bought at the above ATAC offices and at all tobacconist's shops.

Trains

Termini is Rome's main line railway station but a very few express trains start from the suburban stations of Tiburtina and Ostiense. Remember that the Italian for an express train is *rapido*. There are English speaking information clerks on duty 0800-2100 at Termini for timetable enquiries. You can also telephone 4775 (although the number is usually engaged). Seats on most trains from Termini can be reserved by telephone by dialling 110.

Taxis

Taxi ranks are clearly marked all over the city and cabs are all painted a distinctive yellow. The meter price is now subject to a supplement, which should be detailed inside the cab. Further supplements are due for night service and at weekends. A fixed fare operates to and from Fiumicino and Ciampino airports – enquire what it is *before* embarking on your taxi ride. There is an efficient 24-hour radio taxi service available by calling 3570 or 3875. Give your telephone number as well as your address. You can also call cabs from the nearest taxi rank, see list of numbers in the Pagine Gialle (Yellow Pages) of the Telephone Directory. Tip up to 15 per cent. Beware of drivers who shortchange or overcharge foreigners. If you suspect you have fallen victim to this brand of fraud, do not hesitate to call a policeman.

Car Rental

Hertz 26, Via Sallustiana, tel: 463334. Avis 1, Piazza Esquilino, tel: 4701. Maggiore 8, Via Po, tel: 869392. Ducci 21, Via Antonio Bosio tel: 860543 (cars with driver/interpreters). In order to hire a self drive car, you will need a current driving licence of your own country. Most car rental companies accept main international credit cards for the deposit. You are strongly advised to take out maximum insurance cover offered for both the vehicle and the passengers.

Motoring Organizations

The Automobile Club di Roma is at 261, Via Cristoforo Colombo (on the way to EUR) tel: 5106. They will answer all motoring enquiries. The Automobile Club also mans a 24-hour assistance centre tel: 5110510. The ACI (Italian Automobile Club) runs a 24-hour breakdown service – tel: 116. Foreign tourists travelling in their own foreign registered cars are entitled to have their vehicle towed to the nearest fully equipped garage for a small concessionary fee. Tourists in possession of the road service card of the Alliance Internationale de Tourisme (AIT) or the Fédération Internationale de l'Automobile (FIA) pay nothing.

Rules of the Road

Few Romans respect the rules of the road to the letter. You will probably frequently encounter cars which ignore and anticipate red lights at intersections so drive with extra caution, remembering that although as in other continental countries priority is given to traffic coming from the *right*, this rule is not always respected. Parking is restricted in the historic centre between 0830 and 1700. Speed limit in force in urban areas is 80km/50mi per hour. Italy is backwards in comparison with the rest of Europe in safety legislation – the compulsory wearing of seat belts, and of crash helmets by motorcyclists, and in police breathalyser tests for drunken drivers. But new draft legislation is in the pipeline and a new Road Safety Code is due to come into force in 1983.

Breakdown

The ACI Breakdown Service (telephone 116) will tow you to one of their authorized repair garages. It is advisable to get an estimate (*preventivo*) before getting repair work carried out. It would be wise to take out comprehensive breakdown insurance (which should include repatriation of the car in case of major accident or breakdown) *before* leaving home. All major foreign car manufacturers have authorized spares centres and repair garages in Rome. For a complete list consult the ACI.

Bicycle rental

R. Collalti's bicycle shop at 82, Via del Pellegrino hires out pedal-cycles. Scoot-a-long, 302, Via Cavour, (tel: 6780206) hires out motor scooters. Minimum age 18 years. Take your passport.

River Travel

During July and August, a private Association called Amici del Tevere runs river trips to the mouth of the Tiber at Ostia and in central Rome. Details in *This Week In Rome*. There are no regular riverboat services.

Carozze

The horse-drawn carriage may be a dying form of transport, but it is still popular among tourists and you can still find about 60 stalwart cab drivers who are prepared to brave the maelstrom of Rome's motor traffic and ply for hire. They gather at Piazza Venezia and in the Piazza S. Pietro. Fares should be bargained in advance. They can be high in comparison with an ordinary cab, but the experience can be beyond price.

Guides

You can hire a qualified English speaking guide for a half or whole day through the Sindacato Nazionale Guide Turistiche, 12 Rampa Mignanelli, tel: 6789842. The fee covers up to 12 persons.

Information

Ente Provinciale per il Turismo (EPT) the Provincial Tourist Board, 11, Via Parigi (near the Grand Hotel) Tel: 461851, will provide wide ranging information on all travel problems. The EPT also has offices at Termini Railway Station (tel: 465461 and 4750078) and, if you are approaching Rome along the motorway, at the Salaria Ovest Service Area as you are approaching the city from Florence, and at the Frascati Est Service Area as you arrive in Rome from Naples.

The leading Italian Travel Agency CIT, 64, Piazza della Repubblica, Tel: 479041 and American Express, 38 Piazza di Spagna Tel: 6764 organize guided excursions in and around the city.

SHOPPING

The traditional best buys in Rome remain the same – leatherwork, including shoes, handbags, belts and travel goods, costume jewellery, high fashion (cheaper than Paris) and women's and men's ready-to-wear clothes (cheaper than London). Most stores and shops will try to cope with non-Italian speakers – don't be embarrassed and above all don't be scared to bargain. It is the custom here to bargain for many transactions, although not where you see 'prezzi fissi' (fixed prices). Practically all commercial activity comes to a halt between 1300 and 1630 for lunch and siesta. Non-food shops tend to close on Monday mornings and food shops on Thursday afternoons, except during the summer months of June, July and August when all shops take their half day on Saturday afternoons.

Most shops in Rome are small family affairs, following the long traditions of individual artisan enterprise, dating back to antiquity. There is unfortunately a tendency these days for old established specialist shops in the city centre to be squeezed out by fast selling boutiques specializing in bags and jeans and pop gear.

The list of shops below is a purely personal selection of tradesmen who have given good service – there are surely many thousands more left to discover: try the Pagine Gialle (Yellow Pages) of the telephone directory, if you need to buy something and don't know where to look.

Shops

Alinari, 98 Via del Babuino; photographs of Old Rome.
Ars Bibendi, 42 Via della Panetteria; good wineshop.
Bella Coppia, Via dei Coronari; excellent selection Italian ceramics and pottery
Bulgari, Via Condotti; *the* jewellers of Rome.
Banditelli, 24 Via dell'Archetto; bookbinders.
Cantini Castoro, Via Due Macelli and Via Torre Argentina; ironmongers.
Carmignani, Via Colonna Antonina; smoker's requisites and interesting gifts.
Collucci, 14 Via S.Maria in Via; photographic materials and processing.
Dotti, 14 Via Cardello; antiquarian bookseller.
Ezio & Fulvio, 6, Corso Rinascimento; ladies hairdresser. Tel: 6543698.
Femme Sistina, 75 Via Sistina; ladies' hairdresser, expensive but good. Tel: 6780260.
Gucci, 8, Via Condotti, the classic bag, scarf and leather shop.
Lion Bookshop, 181 Via del Babuino; English books.
Nazzareno Gabrieli, Piazza S.Andrea delle Fratte; Luxury leather goods and accessories.
Ricordi, 506 Via del Corso and Via Battisti, near Piazza Venezia; records.
Valentino, 24 Via Gregoriana; high fashion.
Vertecchi, Via della Croce; stationery, wrapping paper, artists' materials.

Department Stores

Coin, Piazzale Appio (general);
Rinascente, Piazza Colonna (clothing and accessories); **Rinascente**, Piazza Fiume (all other household goods)
Standa, 379, Via del Corso (Marks & Spencers type of store)
Standa, 173 Via Cola di Rienzo (this one has a food department)
Tebro, 46/56 Via dei Prefetti (men's and women's clothing and household goods)
Upim, 172 Via del Tritone (Marks & Spencers type of store. This one has a food dept)
Upim, 211 Via Nazionale (Marks & Spencers type of store. This one has a food dept)

Shopping Streets Via Condotti, which runs from the Via del Corso to Piazza di Spagna is Rome's Bond Street. There are good shoe and clothing shops in several of the streets running parallel i.e. Via della Croce, Via Bargognona, and Via Frattina.

The Via dei Coronari is the centre for antique shops – but most of the antiques now come from the Portobello Road in London!

Prati, the quarter north of the Vatican, is a good shopping area. Prices are lower than in the city centre and there is a wider choice of goods. Try particularly the Via Cola di Rienzo.

Markets

Colourful food markets are held daily, except Sundays, in the Piazza Campo dei Fiori, in the Piazza Vittorio Emanuele (near Termini Railway Station) and in Prati near the Via Trionfale. But the classic Rome market is held on Sunday mornings at the Porta Portese. You can buy almost anything there, but go early and avoid the pickpockets!

FOOD & DRINK

It is advisable not to come to Rome and expect what you eat at home. Food is good in Italy but keep to Italian specialities. Nothing is more shocking to an Italian restaurant-owner than to see foreigners insisting on eating *la pasta* with their meat, or salad with their ice-cream. Again, "In Rome do as the Romans". You will be respected and well treated in an Italian restaurant if you respect traditional Italian cooking and eating. Always show some trust in the owner's or waiter's suggestions.

Trattoria is the Italian name for restaurant. It comes from the verb *trattare*, to treat. So, have a good treat! You will find the name *ristorante* in Rome but it can be slightly more pretentious, certainly more expensive and not necessarily better. It is hard not to eat well in Rome but it is easy to be cheated. So, first advice is to avoid eating in tourist places. Avoid 'tourist' menus and mainly areas around the Vatican, the railway station, the Pantheon and Piazza Navona. Go for hidden trattorias in small *vicolos* (small streets off the main track) you will have the pleasure of discovering small and genuine eating-places with a real Roman atmosphere not to be missed. And do not be afraid to waste your time wandering in Rome, there is always something round the corner worth seeing and next to it a

Duty-free allowances for UK residents *subject to change*		Goods bought in a duty-free shop	Goods bought in EEC
Tobacco	Cigarettes	200	300
	or		
	Cigars *small*	100	150
	or		
	Cigars *large*	50	75
	or		
	Pipe tobacco	250 gm	400 gm
Alcohol	Spirits *over 38.8° proof*	1 litre	1½ litres
	or		
	Fortified or sparkling wine	2 litres	3 litres
	plus		
	Table wine	2 litres	4 litres
Perfume		50 gm	75 gm
Toilet water		250 cc	375 cc
Other goods		£28	£120

US customs permit duty-free $300 retail value
of purchases per person, 1 quart of liquor per person over 21,
and 100 cigars per person.

trattoria. You will soon find out by the crowded restaurants in Rome that eating is one of the most serious activities in this town. Here people take their time to have lunch as they often have a siesta (sleep) after.

You will also find out that you cannot face an Italian lunch if you are sightseeing in the afternoon. So, good advice is not to sit in a restaurant for a one-course meal. In Rome it is considered ill-mannered, it would cost you more than you think and you will not really enjoy the atmosphere of a good meal in a Roman trattoria. If you only want a break for lunch, all the bars of Rome will provide you with delicious sandwiches, fresh and varied, a glass of wine, and other drinks, plus coffee, of course. Keep your free time for a real meal of three courses in a restaurant. You can also have a little more than a sandwich at a *tavola calda*, which is the equivalent of a snack bar and provides freshly prepared dishes of the day that you can eat in a hurry. This is cheaper than a restaurant but, of course, second class quality in cooking.

Booking a table at a trattoria in Rome is only essential if you have a large party, more than four, and on Saturday nights. Otherwise it is not the custom here. Saturday night is not an ideal evening for a good meal as everywhere is crowded and the service obviously mediocre. For the same reasons avoid Sunday lunch-time. Have a picnic instead.

How to 'do as the Romans do'

In order to 'do as the Romans do' in a trattoria always ask first for *la carta* and the wine list where prices are listed. And always check twice on your bill. Unlike in France, a set menu is not traditional here. After having read *la carta* ask your waiter for his suggestions. A key question in an Italian restaurant is, *Ché cosa c'è oggi?*, What is there today? Allow yourself to be guided, Italian waiters take pride in their job and it is part of the game.

Usually, a first course is either *antipasto*, smoked ham, salami, cold vegetables, well prepared, etc. or the traditional pasta.

There the choice is vast. Be curious and daring. *Il secondo* or second course is either meat or fish. Vegetables or *contorno* are never served with meat if not ordered. You can let yourself be tempted as fresh vegetables, raw or cooked, are always first class quality and fresh in Rome. Choose according to season. Fresh mixed salads are excellent. A third course is either fruit, and there the choice is attractive for all seasons, or a variety of sweets and delicious ice-creams. Go for home-made ice-creams, they are the best. You can also have cheese but you will definitely shock the Romans if you have it after your sweet. Four price ranges are used to categorize restaurants in Rome. At the time of writing with the lira at 2050=£1 and 850=$ the range is from *inexpensive*; 10,000 lira per head (about £5 or $12), through *moderate*; 15,000, to *expensive*; 20,000 plus and *very expensive or luxurious*; 30,000–50,000 plus.

Wines are excellent in Italy and much cheaper than in France. Beware of carafe wine, often now adulterated except in first-class restaurants. Spend a little more on a bottled wine and drink less, and you will avoid headaches. The choice in white and red bottled wine is rich. Ask the waiter to help you choose with the wine list, and according to your means and taste you will find what suits you.

Any white from Orvieto or Frascati is good. Any red from Tuscany (chianti), Umbria and the North of Italy is good. Tap water in Rome tends to be rich in chlorine, so do as the Romans do, drink mineral water either flat or fizzy.

Any bar and trattoria in Rome will serve you alcohol and soft drinks. Scotch here is cheaper than in Britain. Do not touch Italian Scotch or brandy, they are beastly. But accept at the end of a meal, a 'digestivo', often offered by the house, which is Italian-made liqueur. Grappa is the equivalent of French Aquavit and very strong. Sambucca is made of aniseed and served with coffee grains, a delicious mixture. Ask for *la mosca*, or the fly, if you want the coffee grains in your drink. Other liqueurs made from various plants are available.

In Rome, if you are dissatisfied with your meal, your wine, the bill, you can and must complain. Usually, the owner will do his best and very naturally will change your wine, or your meat and will really try to satisfy his customer. Again, this is because eating is taken seriously and with pride in this country. Check your bill carefully. You can pay cash and most places accept international credit cards. A service charge of 10–15 per cent will be added to your bill but you should also tip the waiter,

and the wine waiter, as they will certainly have been attentive and helpful. You can reckon on adding 30 per cent to your bill. Never tip the owner, you will offend him.

Fish restaurants

Being so near to the sea you can eat fresh fish in Rome, but you can be cheated on fish as on anything else. If you decide to eat fish and seafood (seafood is not recommended in months of peak heat, July and August, and, according to latin tradition, not outside months with an 'R') *always* ask to see and choose your fish before letting it be cooked. If you arrive in time for lunch or dinner at Leonardo da Vinci Airport, Fiumicino, the fishing port of Rome, (ten minutes away) is ideal. You can sit out in the sun by the seaside or along the jetty and enjoy the sight of fishing boats and yachts going out to sea or coming back. And, of course, there you will find first class fresh fish. Almost every restaurant along the jetty offers good food. *Do not leave your bags and suitcases in your car.*

Three recommended restaurants in Fiumicino:

Il Molo: 1st class. Very well situated with inside and outside 180° view over the sea. (6440118) closed on Monday. Moderate.

La Perla: 1st class, same value as above, terrace outside with view of the jetty. (6440038)

Both restaurants have excellent risotto, fish, sea-food, etc.

Capo Grossi: 2nd class, cheaper but good quality fish, seafood, pasta and risotto. Charming shady terrace overlooking the jetty. Inexpensive.

All three restaurants, among others to your choice and fancy are situated in Via Torre Clementina along the jetty. No need to reserve. As for closing days apart from Il Molo, they vary according to season, shortage of staff, strikes, etc., but do not get discouraged, just go. Most restaurants in southern Italy are open late in the afternoon and night.

Roman fish restaurants

Alvaro Al Circo Massimo Via dei Cerchi 53 (6786112) (1st class) Best and freshest fish in town plus great Roman atmosphere and superb wines. Try *Rapitala* or *Torgiano bianco*. Ask Alvaro (the owner) to choose for you according to your tastes. Alvaro's other speciality is game in season. Moderate.

In Trastevere (a typical and oldest part of Rome) you can pick and choose along

CONVERSIONS
CLOTHING
Shoes

Men's	British	6	7	8	9	10
	European	40	41	42	43	44
	USA	6½	7½	8½	9½	10½
Women's	British	4	5	6	7	8
	European	36	37	38	39	40
	USA	5½	6½	7½	8½	9½

Dresses

British	10/32	12/34	14/36	16/38	18/40
European	42	44	46	48	50
USA	8	10	12	14	16

Men's Collar Sizes

British/USA	14	14½	15	15½	16	16½	17
European	36	37	38	39	41	42	43

TEMPERATURES

C°	20	10	0	10	20	30	40	50
F°	20		0	32 40	60	80	100	120

WEIGHT

		($\frac{1}{4}$ kg)	($\frac{1}{2}$ kg)	($\frac{3}{4}$ kg)	(1 kg)
Grams	50 100 150 200 250 300	400	500	600 700 750 800 900 1000	
Ounces	0 1 2 3 4 6 8 12	16	24	32	36
	($\frac{1}{4}$ lb) ($\frac{1}{2}$ lb)	(1 lb)	(1½ lb)	(2 lb)	(2¼ lb)

FLUID MEASURES

litres	0	5	10	20	30	40	50
imp. gals	0			5		10	
US gals	0			5		10	

LENGTH

cm	0	5	10	15	20	25	30
inches	0	2	4	6	8	10	12
metre	0			1m			2m
ft/yd	0	1ft		1yd		2yd	

DISTANCE

km	0	1	2	3	4	5	6	8	10	12	14	16
miles	0	½	1	1½	2	3	4	5	6	7	8	9	10

Via della Lungaretta starting from Piazza Santa Maria in Trastevere to Viale Trastevere.

Antica Pesa Via Garibaldi 18 (5809236)
Excellent fish and Roman cuisine. Inside garden, quite romantic on warm evenings. Very expensive.

Arco Di S. Calisto Via dell'Arco di San Calisto, 45 (588323) (Piazza Santa Maria in Trastevere)
Excellent fish and Roman Cuisine. Very expensive.

Carlo Piazza Mastai 16B (5810244)
Fish and Roman cuisine good and expensive.

Da Gino Via della Lungaretta 85 (5803403)
Fish and Roman cuisine. Moderate.

Galeassi Piazza Santa Maria in Trastevere 3 (5809009)
Fish and Roman cuisine. Expensive.

Sabatini Piazza Santa Maria 13 (582026)
Fish and Roman cuisine. Good but slightly pretentious. Expensive.

I have personal experience of these fish restaurants in Rome and recommend a visit. Obviously, there are many more, Rome being a city of churches and trattorias, but they won't be cheaper than the ones cited above for the good reason that *fish and steak* are and have always been very expensive in Rome. Do not rely too much on the value of the meals indicated above. Inflation is going at the rate of 20 per cent in Italy and the value of your meal will depend on what you eat and choose. Fish is charged according to weight and species. Crayfish is always a luxury. You won't get fish and chips in Rome (thank God for that). Mediterranean fish is something exquisite and quite enjoyable in the sun with white wine. Too many people have discovered that truth. Fish is rarer and dearer.

For the 'expert' gastronome, the cuisine of Rome is neither as good as that in the North nor yet as bad as that in the South! But there is a wide choice of regional cuisine in Rome from *Cucina Bolognese*, *Cucina Toscana* and *Pizzeria Napolitana*.

Here is a choice of the most expensive restaurants in Rome, there are many more. Here again, prices vary according to inflation, your choice of specialities. On price lists beware of 'S.G.', which means 'according to size', usually for lobster, fish and beef. So settle the matter with the restaurateur beforehand if you do not want him to charge you what he feels like.

Al Chianti Via Ancona 17 (861083)
Tuscan specialities of game, grilled meat and Chianti wines. Very expensive

Alfredo Imperatore Piazza Augusto Imperatore, 30 (6781072)
Specialism of fettucine al triplo burro (pasta with triple butter) manipulated by the owner with original servers of gold given to him by the film stars Douglas Fairbanks and Mary Pickford. Very expensive.

Al Moro Vicolo delle Bollette 13 (6783495)
Essential to book. Specialities; Spaghetti Moro, Abbachio arrosto (roast lamb). Very expensive.

Cannavoto Piazza San Giovanni in Laterano 20 (775007)
Specialities: Rigatoni alla Rigoré, Veal scallop in wine. Moderate.

Dal Bolognese Piazza del Popolo 1 (380248)
Specialities: Bolognese, Tortellini alla panna (pasta with cream). Elegant, crowded and expensive but good.

Domus Aurea nel Parco del Viale del monte Oppio (7315325)
Various specialities of pasta and fish. Dancing evenings, orchestra. Elegant and superb view of the Colosseum. Luxury.

El Toula Via della Lupa 29 (681796)
Booking essential. Specialities: Risottos, kidneys with rosemary, sorbets. Luxury.

Georges Via Marche 7 (484575)
Small, intimate. Booking essential. Various specialities. Luxury.

Hosteria Dell'Orso Via Monte Brianzo 93 (6564250)
Booking essential. Most elegant setting in medieval palace, night club (closed lunch time). Luxury.

Mastrostefano Piazza Navona 94 (6541669)
Elegant, modern beautiful setting, outside terrace overlooking Bernini fountains. Speciality: grilled wild mushrooms in season. Expensive.

Passetto Via Zanardelli 14 (6543696)
Specialities: Pasta with cream and mushrooms, veal maison. Expensive.

Ranieri Via Mario dei Fiori (6791592)
Booking essential. Small, intimate. Founded a century ago by Queen Victoria's chef Giuseppe Ranieri. Specialities: Crêpes alla Ranieri, mignonnettes Regina Vittoria. Expensive.

Severino Piazza Zama 5c (750872)
Specialities: pasta, lamb and veal. Expensive.

The White Elephant Via Aurora 19 (483718)
Booking essential. Smart, very expensive, various specialities. Luxury.
Closing days vary each year. Most restaurants are closed in August. So, better check by telephone first.

The following lists select restaurants according to districts and include those in every category.

Piazza del Popolo, Ripetta, Corso, Babuino, Piazza di Spagna

Alfredo Imperatore cf. above

Antico Bottaro Passaggiata di Ripetta 15 (683318)
Lamb and pasta. Moderate.

Augustea Via della Frezza 5 (6784628)
Fish. Moderate.

Dal Bolognese cf. above.

La Berninetta Via Belsiana 58 (6792082)
Fish, risotto and mushrooms. Expensive.

Le bistrot de Paris Via dei Greci 5 (6793284)
French and International. Expensive.

Nino a Via Borgognona Via Borgognona 11 (6795676)
Pasta and tuscan specialities. Florentine steak. Expensive.

Otello alla Concordia Via della Croce 81 (6791178)
Artichokes, cannelloni and pasta. Moderate.

Ranieri cf. above

Toto alle Carrozze Via della Carrozze 10 (6785558)
Artichokes and other Roman specialities. Moderate.

This area of Rome being the elegant center or equivalent of Mayfair area in London is obviously one of the most expensive.

Piazza Navona, Pantheon, Piazza Colonna

Alfredo Alla Scrofa Via della Scrofa, 104 (6540163)
Pasta and poultry. Expensive.

Biblioteca della Valle Largo Teatro Valle, 7 (6541292)
Pasta, veal and pizzeria. Closed at lunch-time. Dinner dancing. Essential to book. Expensive.

El Toula cf. above.

Il Buco Via Sant'Ignazio 8 (6793298)
Tuscan specialities. Expensive.

La Campana Vicolo della Campana 18 (655273)
Roman specialities.: pasta, artichokes, roast lamb. Moderate.

La Fontanella Largo Fontanella di Borghese 86 (6783849)
Crepes al formaggio and tuscan specialities. Expensive.

L'Eau Vive Via Monterone 85 (6541095)
French and international. Expensive.

Osteria dell'Antiquario Piazzetta di San Simone 27 (659694)
Roman specialities: spaghetti, veal and lamb. Moderate.

31 Al Vicario Via degli Uffici del Vicario 5 (6792251)

Rice, pasta and crepes. Expensive.

Tre Scalini (with bar) Piazza Navona 28–30 (659148)
Cannelloni, pasta and ice-creams. Moderate.

Campo dei Fiori, Largo Argentina, Campidoglio

Angelino a Tormagna Piazza Margana 37 (6783428)
Pasta and poultry. Expensive.

Da Gigetto al Portico d'Ottavia Via Portico d'Ottavia 21 (6561105)
Artichokes, beef and fish. Moderate.

Filetti di Baccala Largo dei Librari 88 (6564018)
Anchovies, fish, salami, pasta. Moderate.

La Carbonara Campo de Fiori 23 (6564783)
Roman specialities. Moderate.

Pancrazio Piazza del Biscione 92 (6561246)
Risotto, pasta, grilled shrimps. Moderate.

Piperno a Monte Cenci Monte Cenci 9 (6540629)
Home made pasta, artichokes, Roman specialities. Moderate.

Settimio Via del Pellegrino, 117 (651978) Roman specialities. Moderate.

Vecchia Roma Piazza Campitelli, 18 (6564604)
Risotto, wild goat, mushrooms. Moderate.

Imperial Forums – Colosseum

Al Gladiatore Piazza del Colosseo 5a (736276)
Roman specialities. Moderate.

Domus Aurea Cf. above.

Taberna Ulpia Piazza Foro Traiano, 2 (689980)
Ravioli alla Traiano, Roman specialities. Moderate.

Tana del Grillo Salita del Grillo, 6b (6798705)
Maccheroni with truffles. Expensive.

Aventino, Testaccio

Apuleius sul Colle Aventino Via Tempio di Diana 15 (572160)
Oysters, fish, shrimps. Expensive.

Checchino Via Monte Testaccio, 30 (576318)
Roman specialities of liver, brains, tripe, etc. Moderate.

Perilli a Testaccio Via Marmorata 39 (572415)
Roman specialities of brains, liver, tripe, etc. Moderate.

Lateran, Appia Antica

Cecilia Metella Via Appia Antica 125 (5110213)
Pasta and grilled chicken. Moderate.

Charly's Saucière Via San Giovanni in Laterano, 268 (736666)
French and International. Expensive.

Da Severino Piazza Zama 5c (750872)
Pasta and Roman lamb. Expensive.

L'Archeologia Via Appia Antica 139 (7880494)
Roman specialities, pasta and grilled chicken. Moderate.

Orazio Via Porta Latina 5 (751201)
Crepes, risotto, roast meat. Expensive.

Severino a Santa Croce Via di Santa Croce in Gerusalemme 1 (750112)
Spinach pasta, rabbit. Expensive.

Island, Trastevere, Janiculum

Checcho er Carrettiere Via Benedetta 10 (5817018)
Fish, spaghetti, roast lamb. Expensive.

Comparone Piazza in Piscinula 47 (5816249)
Oxtail, lamb, various pasta. Moderate.

Corsetti: Il Galeone Piazza San Cosimato 27 (5809009)
Roman specialities and fish. Expensive.

Paris Piazza San Calisto 7/a (585378)
Fish, pasta, fillet steak. Expensive.

Pastarellaro di Severino Via San Crisogono 33 (5810871)
Pasta, hare in season, veal. Moderate.

Romolo a Porto Settimiana Via di Porta Settimiana, 8 (588284)
With garden where it is said that Raffaello met and portrayed la Fornarina, Roman specialities. Moderate.

Scarpone Via San Pancrazio 15 (5890094)
Pasta alla Garibaldi, sauté al Gianicolo. Moderate.

Sora Lella Via Ponte Quattro Capi; 16 (Isola Tiberina) (6369907)
Pasta, roast lamb, artichokes. Moderate.

Taverna Trilussa Via della Pliteama 23 (588918)
Rigatoni, turkey and veal. Moderate.

Vincenzo alla Lungaretta Via della Lungaretta 173 (585302)
Fish and fish soup. Moderate.

Borgo-San Pietro, Prati, Monte Mario

Alfredo a San Pietro Via dei Corridori 60 (6569554)
Pasta, veal. Expensive.

Antico Falcone Via Trionfale 6 (353400)
Pasta, ravioli, lamb. Moderate.

Brigadoon Via Aurelia 12 (6900009)
Special grills. Expensive.

Il Matriciano Via dei Gracchi 55 (355247)
Roman speciality. Moderate.

Nino alla Camilluccia Via della Camilluccia 60 (340829)
Pasta, lamb chicken. Expensive.

Pierdonati Via della Conciliazione 39 (6543557)

Beef, veal and pasta. Moderate.

Tritone, Fontana di Trevi

Abruzzi Piazza Santi Apostoli
Fettucine doppio burro, roast beef, fish. Moderate.

Colline Emiliane Via degli Avignonesi, 22 (476538)
Bologna specialities and truffles. Moderate.

Gino Via Rasella 52 (460457)
Bistecca alla fiorentina, zuppa di fagioli. Moderate.

(In Via Rasella, during the Second World War, a Nazi commando was attacked by Roman partisans. In reprisals, 350 Romans including children were shot in the *Cave Ardeatine* along the Via Ardeatina.)

Gioia mia, Pisciapiano Via degli Avignonesi 34 (462784)
Roman specialities and pizzeria, Pizza alla televisione. Moderate.

Sergio e Ada Via del Boccacio 1 (489284)
Roman specialities, pasta and veal. Moderate.

Tullio Via S; Nicola da Tolentino, 26 (4758564)
Tuscan specialities and game. Expensive.

Via Veneto, Ludovisi, Parioli
This is the most expensive area of Rome. Here restaurants enter the luxury category and are not better and certainly less typical.

Al Ceppo Via Panama 2 (8449696)
Speciality of pasta with truffles and game. Luxury.

Al Fogher Via Tevere 13/b (857032)
Venetian specialities. Luxury.

Ambasciata d'Abruzzo Via Tacchini 26 (878256)
Abruzzi specialities. Luxury.

Cesarina Via Piemonte 109 (460828)
Bologna specialities. Luxury.

George's cf. p. 18

Giggetto il Pescatore Via Sant'Elia (Acqua Acetosa) (879929)
Fish, seafood and Roman specialities. Luxury.

Girrarosto Fiorentino Via Sicilia 44 (460660)
Florentine specialities. Luxury.

St Andrews Via Lazio 22 (464680)
Booking essential. Italian and international specialities and special diets. Luxury.

San Soucis Via Sicilia 20 (460491)
Booking essential. Specialities: pasta and meats. Luxury.

The White Elephant cf. p. 18

Ponte Milvio, Flaminio

Le Coq d'Or Via Flaminia Vecchia 493 (393247)
International. Expensive.

La Fattoria Via Flaminia 14 (6912680)
Roman specialities. Moderate.
La Vigna dei Cardinali Piazzale Ponte Milvio 34 (3965846)
Risottos, pasta, fish. Expensive.
Righetto al Flaminio Via Flaminia 395 (390763)
Fish specialities. Expensive.

Porta Pia, Nomentano

Coriolano Via Ancona 14 (861122)
Ravioli, risottos and fish. Moderate.
Costa Balena Via Messina 5 (857686)
Genoese and Roman specialities. Risottos and fish. Expensive.
Loreto Via Augusto Valenziani, 19 (489286)
Fish specialities. Expensive.
Taverna Flavia Via Flavia 9 (489214)
Risottos, fillet steak. Expensive.

Portuense

Carlo il Verace Via dei Colli Portuensi 5151 (532117)
Risottos, grilled fish and lobsters. Expensive.
Il Fungo all'Eur Piazza Pakista 1 (5911959)
Crespelle di ricotta, various meats. Expensive.

Some suburbs of Rome are residential and do not offer a choice of moderately priced restaurants. In those areas, restaurants tend to be modern, fairly large, with a more or less good service, rarely typical but sometimes quite good. The atmosphere tends to be 'parvenu'.

Unlike Paris, Rome has no tradition of restaurants with shows. But from ancient times Rome has had a tradition of singers and poets coming in the evenings to entertain customers in the trattorias. In most trattorias in the centre, especially in Trastevere, you will, in the evenings and sometimes at lunchtime hear some old Roman or Neapolitan songs and for a moderate tip, you can have a private bel canto at your table. Poets are getting rarer but still perform in some theatre-restaurants of Trastevere. But unless you are initiated to Roman slang, and with the best knowledge of Italian, you risk missing all the jokes and spending a very dull evening. Roman slang, like Cockney, is only understandable to the natives or experts. My advice would be to keep to the trattorias where you can hear Roman songs or to the conventional restaurant-nightclub. Most first class international hotels have panoramic roofgarden restaurants plus a nightclub next door or on some evenings dancing with a special orchestra.

Hotels

Eden Via Ludovisi 49 (4743551)
Roof garden. Expensive.

Forum Via Tor de' Conti 25 (6792446)
Roof garden. Expensive.
Hassler-Villa Medici Piazza Trinita sei Monti 6 (6792651)
Roof garden. The most expensive hotel in Rome.

Restaurants

Csarda Via Magnanapoli, 6 (6796366)
Hungarian restaurant. Gipsy music.
Domus Aurea in the park of the Viale del Monte Oppio (7315325)
Elegant restaurant, superb view of Colosseum. Dancing in evening. Expensive.
Da Fieramosca Piazza de Mercanti, Trastevere (5890289)
Trattoria with musicians. Expensive.
Da Meo Pattaca Piazza de Mercanti 30 (5816198)
As above, typical Trastevere trattoria with musicians. Expensive.
Fantasie Di Trastevere 6, Via di Santa Dorotea (5891671)
Roman restaurant, Roman folk songs and jokes, only for experts. Expensive.
Hosteria Dell'Orso Via dei Soldati 25 (6564250)
One of the gastronomic temples, with night club on the ground floor also opened to outside customers, beautiful Renaissance setting. Only two guitarists performing and a piano bar, relaxing atmosphere. Expensive.
La Cisterna 3–5 Via San Francesco a Ripa (582543), 10–11–12 Via Della Cisterna (5817008)
Waiters and musicians wearing 18th-century Roman costumes, Roman and regional songs. Expensive.
Paradise Via Mario dei Fiori 97 (6784838)
This is the only show in Rome. Here you can drink or dine. Booking essential for dinner, (854459). Expensive.
Romulus Via Salaria 1069 (8401669)
Roman trattoria in the suburbs where you can dine and dance.
Wiener Bierhaus Via della Croce 22 (6795569)
Viennese cooking and musicians. Moderate.

ENTERTAINMENT

Finding out what's on is best tackled from scanning the entertainment pages of the daily press, particularly *la Repubblica* which publishes an exhaustive entertainment supplement each Friday. The best English language guides are *This Week in Rome* and the two English language dailies. Concerts with well known international artistes and performances by distinguished foreign opera troupes or theatre companies get sold out quickly, so get your tickets as early as possible. Booking is not normally possible more than three or four days in advance for theatres and concerts. There is no reliable ticketing agency, but your hotel porter may be able to help.

Theatre

You can usually taste some classic Italian theatre, Goldoni or Pirandello during the winter season, at one of the dozen main theatres in Rome if your Italian is up to it.

The Teatro Sistina in the Via Sistina specialises in revues and musicals. A number of small offbeat theatres (known quaintly in Italian as 'teatri off') have grown up in Trastevere in recent years. They perform exclusively in Italian and for this reason are of limited interest to the foreign visitor.

In July and August there are open air theatre performances in the Roman Theatre at Ostia Antica, and under Tasso's oak tree on the Gianicolo. (Amfiteatro Quercia di Tasso). There is also open air ballet at the Teatro di Verdura in the Villa Celimontana Park.

A new development is the use of circus tents as permanent theatres. Try the Teatro Tenda in the Piazza Mancini, and the Teatro Tenda a Strisce, Via Cristoforo Colombo.·

Opera

Rome's opera house is an unattractive late 19th-century building and the quality of performances tends to be limited by the political manoeuvring of the management, which is an unfortunate fact about the whole opera scene in Italy today. The winter season which normally includes a ballet or two, begins in December and lasts until April. In July and August a summer season of open air opera is held in the magnificent setting of the Terme di Caracalla, but here again there is a snag. Top performers do not like singing late at night in the open air – so look for spectacle rather than for virtuoso performance.

Concerts

Rome lacks a modern concert hall with good acoustics. The Accademia di S. Cecilia, the leading musical organisation in the city gives an annual concert season with many leading international guest artistes at the Auditorio Pio, 4 Via della Conciliazione (near the Vatican). Performances are normally on Sunday afternoons, with a repeat on Monday nights. Chamber music concerts are given at the Accademia's own small concert hall at 18, Via dei Greci. Other chamber concerts are held in a former oratory the Gonfalone, 32a Via del Gonfalone. Orchestral concerts and recitals organised by the Accademia Filarmonica, Via Flamini Nuova 118 are held at the Teatro Olimpico 17 Piazza Gentile da Fabriano. For details see wall hoardings and the daily press. Some excellent recitals and choral concerts are often held inside churches particularly during summer. Details from posters on the outside walls of· main churches in the city centre.

Night clubs

Rome boasts a score of nightclubs ranging from the plushy and expensive, such as La Clef in the Via Marche, to the ear splitting discos of Parioli. Among the better known discotheques are Charlie Club, 6 Via Ferdinando di Savoia, Piper Club, 9, Via Tagliamento, and Scarabocchio 8, Piazza Ponzani. Fantasie di Trastevere, 6, Via S. Dorotea, is a restaurant with floor show much patronised by group tours. There are several jazz clubs including Mississippi Jazz Club, 16 Via Borgo Angelico (Piazza Risorgimento) Basin Street Jazz Bar, Via Aurora 27, and Music-Inn, 3, Largo dei Fiorentini.

Cinema

Rome is no longer the centre of a thriving international film industry as it was during the *dolce vita* days of the 1950s, but cinemagoing is still more popular than in most other European capitals despite the lure of dozens of old films every day on private TV channels. Only one cinema, the Pasquino in Trastevere (tel: 5803622) shows original version films in English; every other cinema in Rome shows films dubbed into Italian. Many small specialist film clubs have spawned in recent years offering repertory seasons of films by well known foreign directors. Details in the daily press, but beware, most of the classic 'oldies' are also dubbed into Italian. Look for the magic letters v.o. to identify a 'versione originale'. In summer open air film shows are given every night in the Via Consolazione, at the back of the Roman Forum.

SPORTS AND ACTIVITIES

Facilities for practising many sports in Rome, including tennis and swimming are often limited to members of private clubs – which means ordinary visitors may be excluded from sporting activities normally available in a big city.

Boating The boating lake at EUR is an ideal centre in summer.

Football (soccer) Italy's most popular sport. Rome boasts two first division teams, Roma and Lazio, and matches are played most Sundays during the season at the Olympic Stadium.

Golf The Olgiata golf course is situated on the Via Cassia, about 20km from the centre. For guest membership apply in writing. The Acqua Santa Golf Course is situated south of Rome 12km/7.5mi along the Via Appia Nuova, tel: 783407.

Greyhound racing on Mondays, Wednesdays and Fridays at Ponte Marconi, 6, Via della Vasca Navale, tel: 566258.

Horseracing Flatracing and steeplechasing at the Cappanelle Racecourse on the Via Appia Nuova, tel: 7990025. Trotting races are held at the Tor di Valle Racecourse, tel: 6564129.

Horse riding Rome Riding Club, 18 Via Monti della Farnesina, tel: 3966214. Tebro Riding Club, 198, Via Tiberina, tel: 6912974.

Jogging The best parks for jogging are the Villa Borghese (central) and the Villa Pamphilj.

Motor racing Local races are held at the Autodromo di Roma, Campagnano di Roma, tel: 9033009.

Sailing Several sailing clubs on the shores of Lago di Bracciano.

Skiing Rome is fortunate in having excellent skiing available in the central Appennine mountains about 2½ hours from the city centre by car. Take the Autostrada towards l'Aquila for Campo Felice and Ovindoli and the Via Salaria for Rieti and Terminillo.

Monte Terminillo 1482–2105m (4862–6906ft) is Rome's nearest and most developed ski resort. 11 skilifts, 2 chairlifts.

Campo Felice 1340–2064m (4396–6772ft) 11 skilifts, 4 chairlifts.

Ovindoli 1375–2220m (4511–7283ft) 7 skilifts, 2 chairlifts.

Newspapers publish daily snow reports.

Sports Centres The Foro Italico was built by Mussolini and expanded for the Rome Olympic Games of 1960. It is under the control of the Italian Olympic Association (called CONI). Beyond Parioli lies the huge Acqua Acetosa Sports Centre which has soccer, rugby, hockey, and polo fields.

Swimming There are indoor and outdoor Olympic-size pools at the Foro Italico, tel: 393625. Hours open to the public are restricted because of official training programmes. At EUR there is an outdoor public pool at Piscina delle Rose, open June-Sept. The best beach for sea-bathing near Rome is at Fregene. Ostia is crowded and polluted and should be avoided.

Tennis Public courts at the Foro Italico, tel: 3966765. Use of most courts in Rome depends on club membership.

Windsurfing An ideal place for the practice of this sport is the Lago di Bracciano.

YOUNG ROME

Rome is a city of pilgrims as well as of tourists, and visitors anxious to economise on the expenses of food and accommodation would do well to examine the possibility of staying in one of the numerous religious institutes which offer simple clean accommodation and cheap food for pilgrims. A complete list can be obtained from the EPT (see under **Accommodation**) but among recommended addresses are the Casa Pallotti, 64 Via dei Pettinari, tel 6568843 and a group of Dutch nuns who run a pensione for foreigners at 20, Via dell'Anima, just behind Piazza Navona.

The main Youth Hostel is at the Foro Italico, 61, Via delle Olimpiade (you have to be a member to stay there). There are many official camping sites around the city, but for convenience sake, in order to avoid wasting time on too much tedious travel through the suburbs, stay as centrally as you can afford.

There are hundreds of ordinary bars in Rome where you can eat a sandwich and buy a glass of wine or beer for a very modest price. The Tavola Calda or snack-bar is another useful eating place for those on a low budget. You can also walk into any small Salsamentaria (grocers shop) and ask the assistant to make you an instant sandwich with a slice or two of salami or mortadella or a piece of cheese, if you wish to picnic in the city.

One of the sights of Rome is the Sunday morning flea market at the Porta Portese (get there early by 0800 if you can) where you can buy practically anything new or secondhand, including books, clothing, archaeological fakes, furniture, boots and shoes, jewellery, records and a vast assortment of bric-à-brac.

Students and foreign visitors can obtain a free pass valid for one year to all State owned museums and galleries in Italy on application to the ENIT office in their country of origin. A small fee is payable for the pass, which is also obtainable in Rome from the Ministero dei Beni Culturali, 18 Piazza del Popplo.

Useful addresses Italian Youth Hostels Association, 61 Lungotevere Maresciallo Cadorna, tel: 3960009. CTS (Youth and Student Tourist Centre) 66 Via Nazionale, tel: 612251. European Student Travel Centre 14, Via S.Agata dei Goti tel: 6785939.

CHILDREN'S ROME

Most Italian newspapers now run a section on their entertainments page devoted to children's activities (*attività per ragazzi*). Group activities for children, other than church-run outings, are still a novelty in Italy, so be tolerant if the organization fails to come up to expectations.

Marionettes are always popular – regular performances at *Marionette al Pantheon*, 32, Via Beato Angelico, tel: 8101887. The *Luna Park* amusement park at EUR which has a Big Dipper and various other excitements is open all the year round. There is a boating lake near the Piscina delle Rose. (Metropolitana to EUR Fermi).

The best ice-cream shop in Rome is *Giolitti* 40, Via Uffici del Vicario (a narrow street near the Parliament building). The **Zoo** (see entry in gazetteer) is always worth a visit while the **Safari Park** near Fiumicino will absorb your children's interest for at least two hours. Over fifty lions and hundreds of monkeys in a beautiful natural setting – you need a car to get there.

Outside Rome, the World Wildlife Fund Bird Sanctuary at La Selva (35km/22mi) provides an interesting day's outing. Take the autostrada towards Naples, turn off at Colleferro, and follow the signs. Open daily except Tuesdays 0930 to sunset. There is an agreeable lakeside trattoria for visitors or on Sundays you can buy and cook your own barbecue (sausages, cheese, bread, fruit and eggs plus local wine).

Visiting practically any of Rome's ancient monuments can be made fascinating for children if the scene is brought to life by a bit of historical background. Most children like the bit about Christians being fed to the lions at the Colosseum.

GENERAL INFORMATION

THEFT is the greatest danger facing visitors to Rome today.
This includes cash, traveller's cheques, luggage, cameras, passports and any possessions you may have with you that are not placed in safe custody. Unfortunately pickpockets, bagsnatchers and luggage thieves make a rich living out of the millions of foreign tourists who now visit Rome every year, and you must take certain basic precautions in order to ensure an enjoyable stay in the city. A visit to any central Rome police station on many days in summer will reveal a distressed queue of foreigners waiting to report the loss of money, baggage or both. *Reduce the risk to a minimum by doing as the Romans do.*
On foot Do not carry cash in a handbag, briefcase, or an outside or back trouser pocket. Never cash more traveller's cheques than you need for your immediate spending. Carry small amounts of cash in the front pocket of jeans, ordinary trousers or skirts. Leave your camera at the hotel unless you actually intend to take photographs. Ask the hotel reception where you should leave passports, traveller's cheques, jewellery and any valuables during your stay in Rome for safe keeping.
In a car Never leave your luggage unattended in a car. This applies not only to the obvious case of luggage fixed to a roof rack, but also to your suitcase hidden in the locked boot (trunk). Do not leave coats, handbags, hand luggage, cassettes, or any other personal items inside your car unless you are paying an attendant to look after it. Always double check that you have left nothing of value in your car before locking it.
In public transport Beware of pickpockets at all times in buses and on the Metropolitana (underground). If despite these precautions, you still get robbed, report the theft immediately to the nearest police station (Pubblica Sicurezza or Carabinieri) and make

denuncia' (official complaint) which you may need in order to make a successful claim on the insurance policy which you will wisely have taken out before you left home.

Do not despair, this is not the first time in history that Rome has become the haunt of robbers. But do remember to observe these basic anti-theft rules and you will be able to set out in a much more relaxed way to visit the city.

Chemists (pharmacies) The following sell English and American proprietary medicines and will dispense foreign prescriptions: Farmacia Internazionale, Piazza Barberini 49 (Tel: 462996); Lepetit, Via del Corso 417 (Tel: 791347); Schirillo, Via Vittorio Veneto 29 (Tel: 493447).

Chemist shops observe the following opening hours: Mon-Fri 0830–1300 and 1630–2000 Sat 0830–1300 Sundays and Public Holidays closed.

Most chemists, even when they are shut, display a list showing the nearest chemists open during the night (2000–0830) and those open uninterruptedly from 0830–2000 daily including Saturdays, Sundays and Public Holidays. Most Rome newspapers publish daily lists of chemists open at night and at weekends. Dial 1921 for a recorded message listing all chemist's shops open outside normal hours in central Rome.

Closing days and times Most museums and galleries are closed on Sunday afternoons and all day Monday except the Vatican museums which are closed all day on Sundays and religious festivals. For individual opening times consult gazetteer. As a general rule few museums are open in the afternoon after 1600 and most close by 1400.

Churches tend to close 1200–1600 daily.

Banks open Mon–Fri 0830–1330. Money change available at Termini Railway Station information office in the main booking hall daily 0800–2100 and at the Leonardo Da Vinci Airport to bona fide travellers 0830–2030.

Shops Non-food. Weekdays 0930–1300 and 1700–1930 or 2000. Closed Monday mornings Sept-April and Saturday afternoons May-Sept.

Food Weekdays 0830–1300 and 1630–1930; Closed Thursday afternoons Sept April and Saturday afternoons May Sept.

Cinemas Three or four separate showings 1630–2230. See newspapers for details. Only cinema where you can see English language films in original version is the Pasquino, 19 Vicola del Piede, Trastevere (Tel: 5803622).

Special feature: sliding roof which means starlight shows on fine nights. **Electricity** standard voltage is now 220V. Continental type plugs and fittings. Bring adaptor for electric razor. **Health** As a member of the EEC Britain has an agreement with Italy that medical advice and treatment will be provided on the same basis as for Italian subjects. British visitors must have certificate E111 indicating entitlement to British National Health Service benefits. This certificate is issued by your local Health and Social Security office after you have completed application form CM1. You should ask for leaflet SA28 which gives details of all the EEC health services. If you need medical aid take certificate E111 to the local sickness insurance office (Instituto nazionale per l'assicurazione contro le malattie) INAM. The INAM office will give you a certificate of entitlement (ask for a list of sickness insurance scheme doctors and dentists). A doctor or dentist will then treat you free of charge. Without the certificate you will have to pay and may have difficulty in obtaining a refund of only part of the costs. Some prescribed medicines are free, others carry a small charge, but you must show form E111 to the chemist.

The doctor will give you a certificate (*proposta di ricovero*) if you need hospital treatment. This entitles you to free treatment in some hospitals. INAM offices have a list. If you cannot contact the INAM office before going into hospital, show form E111 to the hospital authorities and ask them to contact INAM at once.

American visitors should ensure that their own medical insurance is extended to cover them while abroad. Insurance brokers or travel agents will advise and arrange the additional cover.

Although there are more doctors per head of population in Italy than in practically any other country in the world, health standards are far from adequate and the state hospital system is under severe strain through overcrowding and lack of funds. Visitors should therefore make sure that they take out adequate health insurance *before* travelling – to include possible emergency repatriation expenses in case of serious accident or illness.

The best hospital for foreigners in Rome is the Salvator Mundi International Hospital, 66/77 Viale delle Mura Gianicolensi, Tel: 586041. It is run by religious and all the doctors and nurses are highly qualified and speak

Piazza della Rotunda

Piazza della Minerva

good English. General Practitioners and Consultants are available for consultation by appointment and fees are reasonable.

Most hotels can put you in touch immediately with a local English speaking doctor or dentist in case of emergency. If you are taken ill or meet with an accident in the street ask for the *Pronto Soccorso* (First Aid Department) at the nearest city hospital. These are: Policlinico (Tel: 492856); S. Camillo (Tel: 5870); S. Eugenio (Tel: 5925903); S. Filippo (Tel: 330051); S. Giacomo (Tel: 6726); S. Giovanni (Tel: 7578241); S. Spirito (Tel: 6540823).

Although a reciprocal National Health Service insurance agreement exists in Italy for nationals of European Community countries, you are strongly advised to rely on private treatment rather than the State Health Service except when there is no alternative. In case of serious illness or accident make arrangements to return home for treatment if at all possible.

Many visitors to Rome suffer minor stomach upsets, particularly in summer. A light diet, plenty of rest, and perhaps some entero-vioform tablets should set you right. If in doubt, consult a doctor.

Lost Property In case of loss or theft report the facts immediately to the nearest Police Station. In order to reclaim any objects handed in to the Municipal Lost Property Office Via Nicolo Bettoni 1, (Tel: 5816040) you will require a copy of your *denuncia* or declaration to the Police on *carta bollata* (foolscap paper bearing an excise stamp purchaseable at any tobacconist's).

Newspapers and magazines Leading British and European newspapers and magazines can be purchased (usually the day after publication) at most street news-stand kiosks in central Rome; the *International Herald Tribune*, published in Paris and printed in Zurich is normally available on the day of issue from 1400. Two English language daily newspapers are published in Rome; they are the *Daily American* and the *International Daily News*.

Fuel and gas Pumps are open from 0730–1230 and 1530–1930 (1500–1900 October-May) on weekdays and Saturdays and most are closed on Sundays, except on the Autostrada (motorway). Automatic pumps open 24 hours which accept (clean and uncrumpled) 1000 lire notes are identifiable by illuminated signs marked SELF-SERVICE.

Police There are four separate police forces you may come into contact with

in Rome, and it is as well to be able to seek and identify the one you need.

The *Carabinieri* are a para-military national police force with a proud history dating back well beyond the founding of the modern Italian State. They wear a dark blue uniform and peaked cap, and patrol in cars clearly marked CARABINIERI. They are efficient and courteous. (Tel: 212121)

The *Pubblica Sicurezza* (Public Security Force) are the main civil police force. They have their own command structure and organization, but liaise with the Carabinieri. They wear a blue grey uniform and patrol in cars marked POLIZIA. The Questura or police headquarters is at 15 Via S. Vitale (behind the Via Nazionale) where a special office (*ufficio stranieri*) deals with foreigners and their problems. (Tel 4686)

The *Vigili Urbani* (Municipal Police deal with traffic control and all minor local security problems. They wear a distinctive white pith helmet or white peaked cap with a white jacket in summer and blue jacket in winter.

The *Guardia di Finanza* (Customs Police) are on duty at the airport and should be approached on questions relating to customs and exchange control

Remember, under Italian law it is a serious offence to obstruct a police officer in the execution of his duty. An angry altercation with the Law could mean that you end up in jail for the night instead of enjoying a moonlight stroll on the Pincio.

The general emergency telephone number for *all* police services is 113 (Note that Rome telephone number vary between three and seven digits.)

Postal Services The *Palazzo dell' Poste* (main Post Office) is in the Piazza S. Silvestro and is open 0800–2100 Mon.-Fri., 0800–1200 Sat., and is closed Sun. and public holidays. Public telex, telegrams, and international telephones are available at the entrances to the immediate left and right of the main door. Stamps can be bought from any tobacconists if you wish to avoid the queues at the post office. Poste Restante service available.

The Italian postal services are subject to unpredictable delays and many Roman residents have more faith in the ability of the **Vatican Post Office** to despatch mail quickly out of the country. In summer, a mobile post office is parked in St Peter's Square (open 0830–1830 daily except Sun.) when you can buy Vatican City postage stamps and post your mail in a distinct tive blue mailbox (in contrast to the red mailboxes of the Italian postal services). In winter there are two small Vatican City post offices operating at the extreme left and right hand sides of St Peter's Square, by the side of the *Arco delle Campane* (Arch of the Bells) and almost directly below the Pope's study window. The only drawback to posting letters from the Vatican is that you have to fight to buy stamps with the philatelists who normally besiege the Vatican counters.

A final warning: apart from the Palazzo delle Poste and the Post Office at Termini Railway Station, all other post offices in Rome close for the day at 1400 (1200 Sat.).

Public Holidays Banks, shops and offices are closed on the following days: New Year's Day, 6 January (Epiphany), Easter Monday (Good Friday is *not* a public holiday), 25 April (Liberation Day), 1 May (Labour Day), 2 June (National Day), 15 August (Feast of Assumption), 1 November (All Saints), 4 November (Victory Day), 8 December (Immaculate Conception), Christmas Day, 26 December (St Stephen's Day).

Radio and TV Vatican Radio broadcasts a multilingual breakfast news and chat show from 0800 daily on VHF and Medium Wave. The *Daily American* operates a local pop music and news station in English on VHF. The BBC World Service from London and the Voice of America from Washington can usually be picked up (reception is best early in the morning) on any good shortwave transistor in the 19, 25, 31 and 49 metre bands.

The main daily Italian TV newscasts on the State network RAI are at 1330 and 2000 (Channel 1) and 1300 and 1945 (Channel 2).

Telephones Automatic trunk dialling is now available to most countries in Europe and to all parts of Italy from Rome. Direct dialling to the United States and Canada is available to private subscribers. The Italian telephone system is run by SIP and the main public call offices are at: Piazza S. Silvestro (next door to the Palazzo delle Poste) 24 hour service), SIP, Via S. Maria in Via (adjacent to Piazza S. Silvestro) (0800–2145) Termini Railway station (0700–2400), Fiumicino International Airport (0800–2045) Fiumicino national departures (0800–2045).

You can also call anywhere in Europe with 'gettoni' (telephone tokens) which you can buy from any shop, kiosk, bar or restaurant displaying the distinctive yellow telephone dial sign outside. It is often difficult to get change for a 'gettone' so buy a small stock for future use.

SIP is introducing a new magnetic Payphone card which will gradually replace the 'gettone' at all public call boxes. The advantage is that you can check visually the cost and duration of your call and don't risk being cut off in the middle of a conversation when you run out of 'gettoni'. Payphone cards are available in denominations of 2000, 5000 and 9000 lire.

To make intercontinental calls through the operator call 170. Emergencies: call 113; Carabinieri, 212121; Questura (police headquarters), 4686.

The Yellow Pages (Pagine Gialle) section of the Rome Telephone Directory is a mine of useful local information. It contains a complete list of addresses and telephone numbers of the main Carabinieri and police stations in and around Rome. The volume also contains an English translation of the main headings (just before the street gazetteer) and a detailed street guide covering all the suburbs linked to a well printed series of maps of the whole urban area of the city.

If you want to call home quickly without spending a fortune, the best way (if your hotel has direct dialling from the room) may be to dial direct and then ask the person at the other end to call you back. Reverse charge or Collect calls are available through the operator, but they are usually subject to long delay.

Telegrams International and local telegrams can be handed in at any Post Office or dictated from any private telephone (if you have some kind Italian friend patient enough to spell them out letter by letter).

Time In winter Italy is normally one hour ahead of GMT. From April to September, Italy in common with the other member countries of the EEC (except UK) follows daylight saving and moves two hours ahead of GMT. This means that in summer Rome is usually one hour ahead of BST in London, and five hours ahead of New York and Toronto. The exact date of switch-over to daylight saving time in different time zones rarely coincides and it's safer to check in case of doubt.

Tipping A 15 per cent service charge is normally included in hotel and restaurant bills, but it is customary to leave a small extra gratuity to the waiter after a meal. *Servizio compreso* means the tip is included. A small tip is customary when you buy coffee or a drink in a bar. Watch how the locals behave and follow suit if you are in doubt.

A 10 per cent tip is normally adequate for taxis. In the Mediterranean accepting a tip is considered neither infra-dig nor a sign of corruption. Try to do it delicately, however, and do not respond to demands for a tip which you consider amount to extortion.

Toilets Public facilities are frequently inadequate and are certainly less luxurious than in the ancient city. Usually easily identifiable by symbols but for the record the ladies' is *signore* while the gents' is *signori*. If you cannot find a public toilet most bars can oblige in an emergency. In some of the posher places a saucer invites a coin for the lavatory lady.

USEFUL ADDRESSES

Italian State Tourist Office (ENIT) 201, Regent Street, London W1 (01-439 2311); 630, Fifth Avenue, New York NY 10020 (212 245 4822); 500, North Michigan Avenue, Chicago (312 644 0990); 380, Post Street, Suite 801, San Francisco 2. (415 392 6206); 3, Place Villa Marie, Plaza Montréal Store 56, Montreal, Quebec, (514 866 7667); 2, Via Marghera, Rome, (4952751).

Rome Provincial Tourist Board (EPT) 11, Via Parigi, Rome (463748); Information Offices: 5, Via Parigi, Rome (463748); Termini Railway Station (465461) Fiumicino Airport (6011255).

Embassies and Consulates

Australia 215, Via Alessandria, (841241)
Britain 80, Via XX Settembre, (475541 & 4755551)
Canada Embassy 27, Via G.B. de Rossi, (855341/4) Consulate 30, Via Zara (8441841)
Ireland 108, Via del Pozzetto (6782541)
New Zealand 2, Via Zara (8448663)
South Africa Palazzo Phillips, 4, Piazza Monte Grappa (3608441)
United States 121, Via Vittorio Veneto, (4674)

Automobile clubs

Automobile Club d'Italia (ACI): 8, Via Marsala (4998); Touring Club Itliano (TCI): 7a, Via Ovidio (388602)
British Council 20 Via Quattro Fontane. (480059 & 4750018). An excellent English language reference and lending library available. Closed in August.

Churches

Roman Catholic S.Silvestro in Capite, Piazza S. Silvestro, is the main Catholic church in Rome for British people wishing to attend Mass in English. S. Susanna, 14 Via XX Settembre, is the equivalent American church where Mass is celebrated by American priests. **Anglican** All Saints (English) 153, Via del Babuino. St Paul's (American) Via Nazionale.
Church of Scotland 7 Via XX Settembre.
Methodist 38, Via Firenze.
Baptist 3, Viale Ionio.
Salvation Army 42, Via degli Apuli.
Quakers 58, Via Napoli.
Jewish Synagogue Lungotevere Cenci.
Islamic Centre 6, Via Conca.

Air travel

Alitalia reservations (24 hour service) 5454. Fiumicino airport 6012. Ciampino airport 4692. Charter arrivals 600251.

Finally, just in case, *Monte di Pietà*, Rome's Municipal Pawnshop, 2, Pazza del Monte di Pieta, (474841). Most likely the world's most elegant pawnshop (where incidentally regular bargain sales are held of unredeemed pledges). Patronized by Romans from all walks of life. No social slur for being seen entering its marble portal.

ANNUAL EVENTS

January

The feast of the Befana (Epiphany) on 6 January is still joyously celebrated with churchgoing and present-giving. The Christmas toy fair in the Piazza Navona comes to an end on this day with a final spending spree. On January 21 in the Church of S. Agnese off the Via Nomentana, the ancient ceremony of the Blessing of the Lambs is held. The lambs are later presented to the Pope.

February

Carnival time is a pale imitation of the annual merrymaking which used to go on until the last century. But it is still an excuse for dressing up the children and party going.

March/April

Holy Week ceremonies are held in the main basilicas and churches. The Pope leads the *Via Crucis* (Way of the Cross procession at the Colosseum on Good Friday evening. On Easter Sunday he delivers his Easter Blessing and message to the crowds in St Peter's Square.

April
Do not miss the spring flower display, masses of azaleas, on the Spanish Steps all the way up to the Trinità dei Monti Church. In Spring and again in Autumn the nearby Via Margutta is the scene of an open air art exhibition.

May
Rome's International Horse Show takes place in the Piazza di Siena amid the umbrella pines of the Villa Borghese. The show attracts competitors from many countries and it is impossible to imagine a more idyllic setting. The antique dealers of the picturesque Via dei Coronari hold an annual Antiques Fair. The International Tennis Championships take place in the Foro Italico in the last week of May.

May/June
Rome's annual Trade Fair takes place at the exhibition grounds in the Via Cristoforo Colombo. Over 1000 exhibitors.

July/August
Open-air opera inside the Terme di Caracalla. *Aida* by Giuseppe Verdi is the favourite. Open-air concerts and theatre performances are held in courtyards of famous palaces and in the Roman theatre at Ostia Antica. For details see newspapers and *This Week In Rome*.

July
About July 20 the weeklong *Festa di Noiantri* is held in Trastevere. A traditional popular festival which has become somewhat commercialized, but is none the less enjoyable. Many poor residents in Trastevere still move their chairs and tables into the street to eat and to escape the stifling summer heat in their apartments.

August
On August 5, the Feast of the *Madonna of the Snows* is celebrated with a Mass in the Basilica of S. Maria Maggiore. White flower petals are released from the roof of the chapel in commemoration of a miraculous summer snowfall.

Most Romans leave the city for the *Ferragosto* holiday of August 15 giving the tourist the unusual opportunity of seeing Rome as it used to be before it was turned into a huge car park.

December
The Feast of the Immaculate Conception on 8 December is celebrated with a drive through the streets of the city by the Pope, and the climax is the laying of a wreath on the statue of the Madonna on top of the Column near the Piazza di Spagna by the Rome Fire Brigade using an extendable ladder. In the first week of December an interesting international Christmas gift Fair is held at the Palazzo dei Congressi at EUR.

The Pope usually celebrates midnight Mass inside St Peter's Basilica on Christmas Eve and delivers his Christmas Blessing and message from the balcony of the Basilica on Christmas Day. Many Roman churches display elaborate Christmas cribs, some of them dating back hundreds of years.

St Peter's Square, scene of general Papal audiences

Dome of St Peter's Basilica

Fountain in St Peter's Square

Terrace above the portico of St Peter's

View from the dome of St Peter's

VATICAN CITY

The smallest independent sovereign state in the world, whose ruler is the Pope, was set up by international treaty in 1929. It lies on the right bank of the River Tiber, extends for just under ½ sq kl/⅕ sq mi in area, has its own railway station, post office, supermarket, radio station, police force, and astronomical observatory. Apart from the Pope and his household, under 1000 people live in the Vatican City.

The hill known as the *Ager Vaticanus* in Roman times, which was near Nero's Circus, is traditionally believed to have been the burial place of St Peter, the first Pope and Bishop of Rome, about the year AD 67. The first great Christian Basilica of Rome was constructed on this site during the reign of the Emperor Constantine the Great in the 4th century AD and it endured for over a thousand years. The present St Peter's was built during the 16th and early 17th centuries. From the time of the Renaissance onwards, the Vatican Palace became one of the main residences of the Roman Pontiff; after the creation of the anti-clerical unified Italian State in 1870 when the Pope lost his temporal realms, it became his virtual prison for fifty years. The status of Vatican City was finally fixed by the *Lateran Treaty* signed by Mussolini and Pope Pius XI on 11 February 1929. The major basilicas of Rome, the Papal villa at Castelgandolfo and certain other Vatican properties in Rome enjoy the same extraterritorial rights under this Treaty.

The spiritual leader of the world's 800 million Roman Catholics is elected for life by his fellow Cardinals (about 120 in number) who gather in Rome on the death of the Roman Pontiff. The Pope governs the tiny Vatican City State with the help of a small civil service, while the Church administration is in the hands of the *Curia* which is divided up into *Congregations*, the ecclesiastical equivalent of Ministries in civil government. The present Pope, Karol Wojtyla from Cracow in Poland, was elected on 16 October 1978. He was the first non-Italian to be elected Pope for over 450 years and took the name John Paul II.

Papal Audiences are of three kinds, private, special and general. Tickets for the last two are issued by the Prefetto della Casa Pontificia (Prefect of the Papal Household) to whom all applications should be addressed. In Rome, tickets for general audiences are distributed through the Embassy to the Holy

See of the country concerned, and for United States citizens from the Bishops' Office for United States visitors to the Vatican, 30 Via dell'Umiltà (North American College).

In winter audiences are held in the ultra-modern Audience Hall built next to St Peter's by Pier Luigi Nervi and completed in 1971, or inside the Basilica. In spring and autumn, the general audiences take place in the open air in St Peter's Square. In summer, audiences take place at the Pope's summer residence at Castelgandolfo. Wednesday is general audience day.

At midday on Easter Sunday and on Christmas Day the Pope delivers his blessing *Urbi et Orbi* (to the city of Rome and to the World) from the balcony in front of St Peter's Basilica. Every Sunday, when he is in residence, the Pope recites the Angelus prayer and makes a short speech from his study window in the Apostolic Palace overlooking St Peter's Square (second window from the right on the top floor as you look up from the Piazza).

For centuries, Roman Catholic students have come to Rome from all over the world to study for the priesthood. The seminarians attend lectures at the Pontifical Gregorian University, known familiarly as 'the Greg' and live in national colleges, many of them of ancient foundation. The English College, in the Via Monserrato, was founded as a hospice for medieval pilgrims.

There are three entrances to Vatican City. The Arco delle Campane, (Arch of Bells) lies to the left of St Peter's Basilica. The Portone di Bronzo (Bronze Gate) lies to the right of the Basilica under the Bernini Colonnade, while the Cancello di S. Anna (St Anne's Gate) the main entrance for vehicle traffic as well as pedestrians, is in the Via d Porta Angelica to the right of the Basilica. Guided tours of the Vatican Gardens take place three mornings a week. For all information regarding Vatican City apply to Ufficio Informazioni Pellegrini e Turisti (Pilgrim and Tourist Information Office) Piazza S. Pietro, (left hand side of the Piazza just before the Arco delle Campane).

Useful addresses British Legation to the Holy See, 91, Via Condotti, tel 6797479. Irish Embassy to the Holy See, 1, Via G. Medici, tel: 5810777 Canadian Embassy to the Holy See, 4 Via della Conciliazione, tel: 654735 Bishops' Office for United States Visitors to the Vatican, c/o North American College, 30, Via dell'Umiltà, tel 6791443. Vatican Switchboard: 6982

Central Rome Maps

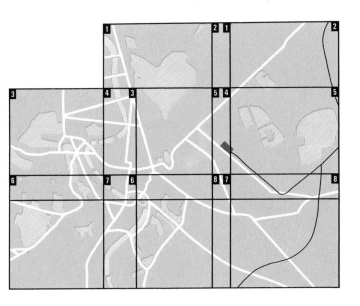

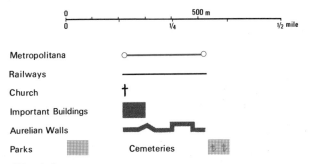

Metropolitana	o——o
Railways	——
Church	†
Important Buildings	■
Aurelian Walls	⌐_⌐
Parks	▦	Cemeteries	▦

Abbreviations

Lgo	Largo/square,	Lung.	Lungotevere/quay,	Mon.	monument
Pal. or Pzo.	Palazzo,	Pass.	promenade,	Ple	Piazzale/large square
Pta	Porta/gate,	Pza	Piazza,	Sal.	Salita/ascent
V.	Via/street,	Vle	Viale/avenue,	Vic.	Vicolo/lane

These maps are adapted with kind permission from the Hallwag city map series

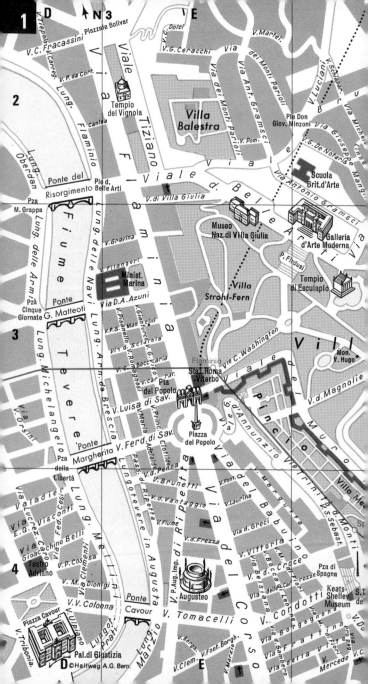

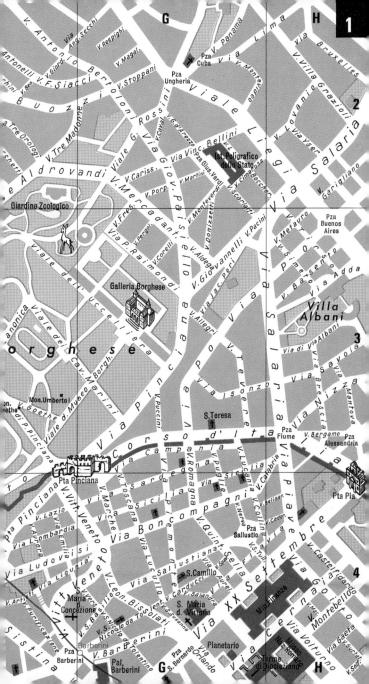

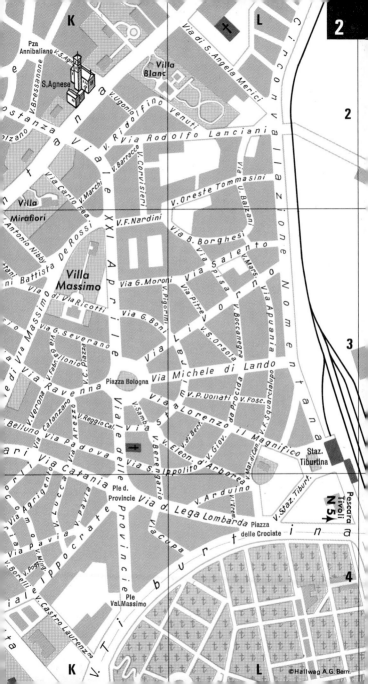

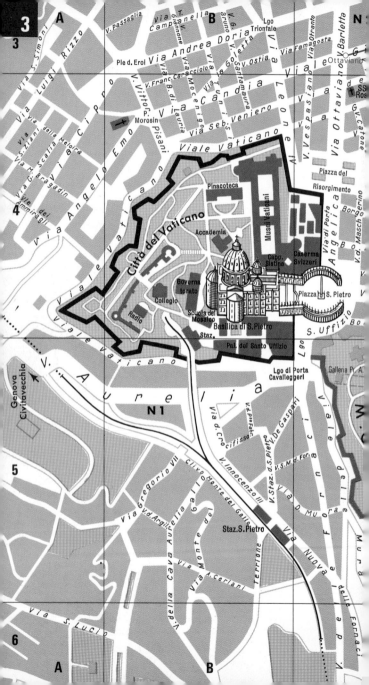

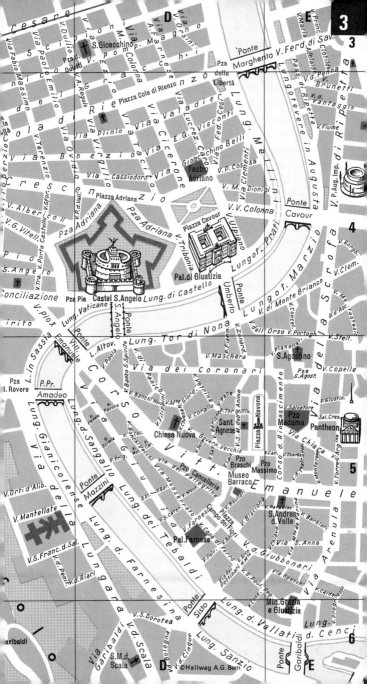

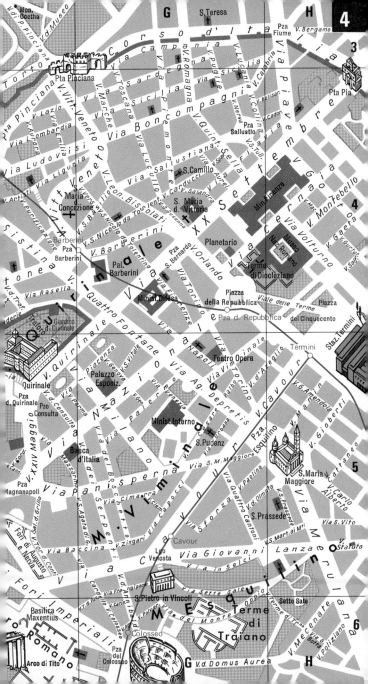

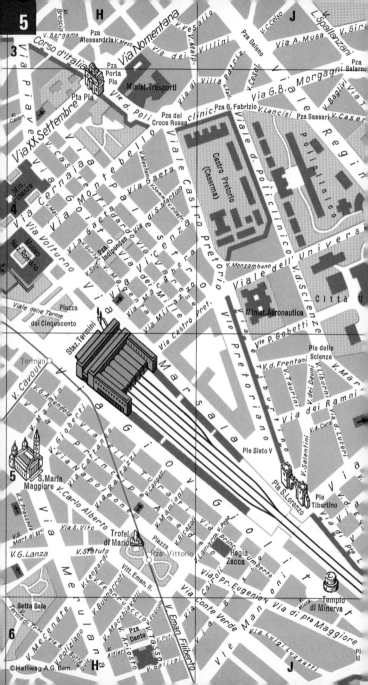

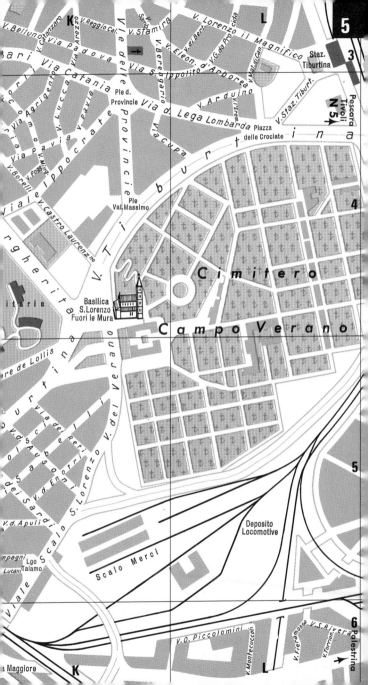

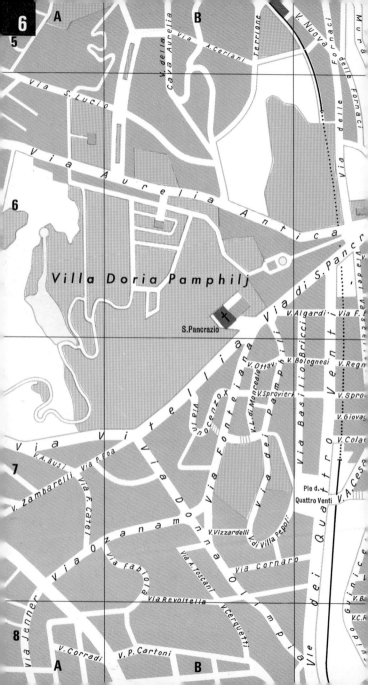

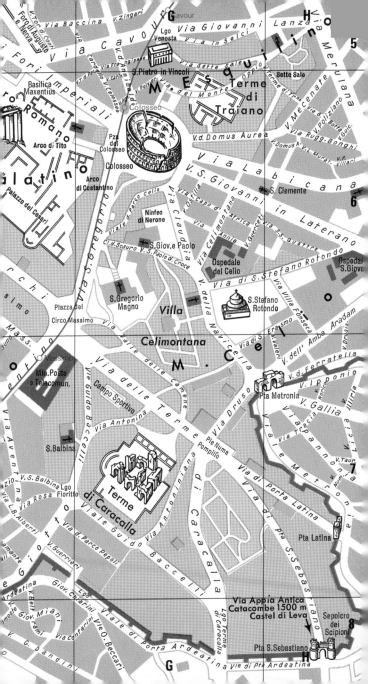

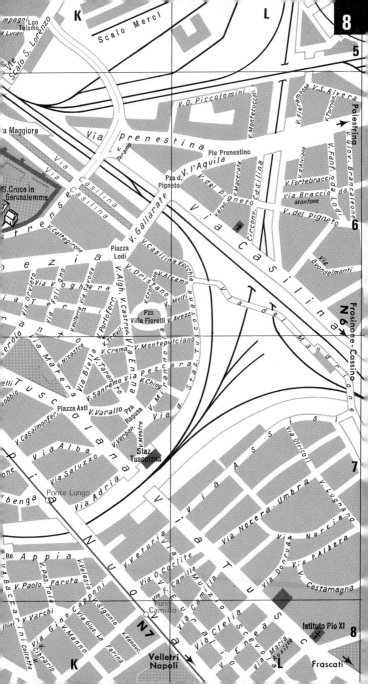

MUSEUMS AND GALLERIES

The wealth and variety of Rome's museums and galleries is only matched by the variety and eccentricity of their opening and closing times. Lack of staff and strikes also sometimes complicate the task of fitting in a museum visit so check times carefully before setting out from your hotel if your time is limited. Broadly speaking, state and communal museums all close on Mondays, New Year's Day, Easter Sunday, May 1, August 15, and Christmas Day, while the Vatican museums are closed on Sundays and all religious feast days. Few museums are open in the afternoon. Those which open on Sundays close early, usually at 1300 sharp.

Museums

Baracco 168, Corso Vittorio Emanuele. A small but fine quality private collection of antique sculpture, Egyptian, Greek, Etruscan and Roman, given to the city of Rome by Baron Baracco at the beginning of the 20th century. It is unusual to find so many Greek originals in a Roman art collection; normally local copies predominate. Tues.-Sat. 0900-1400 closed Mondays and public holidays. Bus 64   3D5

Capitolino Piazza del Campidoglio, Via Teatro di Marcello. The world's oldest public collection of classical sculpture and statuary was begun as a private collection by Pope Sixtus IV in 1474. You reach it by climbing the elegant ramp or *cordinata* originally designed by Michelangelo for the triumphal entry into Rome of the Holy Roman Emperor Charles V in 1536. At the centre of Michelangelo's magnificent piazza stands the equestrian bronze statue of Marcus Aurelius, one of the most dramatic and moving works of art to have survived from the ancient world. Here ancient and Renaissance Rome blend in astonishing harmony. The collection is housed in three palaces, the Palazzo Nuovo on the left, the Palazzo dei Conservatori on the right, and the Palazzo Caffarelli or Museo Nuovo to which you gain access through the Palazzo dei Conservatori.   4E5

Palazzo Nuovo A gigantic river god, Marforio, one of the *speaking statues* of Rome (see p.63) decorates the courtyard fountain. Upstairs is the 'Capitoline Venus' which was dug up in the 17th century – it is a Roman copy of a Greek original from the 2nd century BC. The celebrated 'Dying Gaul' is a copy of a lost Greek bronze of the 3rd century BC. The most fascinating part of the museum is the large collection of Roman portrait busts – Emperors, philosophers and orators line the walls in serried ranks giving you the opportunity to meet face to face, as it were, the political and moral leaders of ancient Rome. The art of portraiture was highly developed, and the austere and determined features of these Romans tell much about the character of the civilization that they imposed on the Europe of their day.

Palazzo dei Conservatori In the courtyard lie the remains – a head, a foot and a hand – of a colossal statue of the Emperor Constantine which once sat enthroned in majesty inside a basilica in the nearby forum. Another fragment of marble bearing the broken inscription BRIT is all that remains of a triumphal arch erected to celebrate Claudius' conquest of Britain in AD 43. Upstairs in the *Sala della Lupa* is one of the most important and beautiful pieces of ancient sculpture in Rome, the 5th-century BC Etruscan bronze of the she-wolf which suckled Romulus and Remus. The twins were added by a Renaissance artist some 2000 years later. Some fine mosaic floors and a superb collection of bronze fragments should not be missed. **Palazzo Cafarelli** is at present undergoing restoration. The garden (not always open) is an oasis of quiet and shade. The museum is one of the very few in Rome which is open and illuminated on Saturday nights and night viewing is to be recommended.
Sun. 0900-1300. Mon. closed. Tues. 0900-1400, 1700-2000. Wed. 0900-1400. Thurs. 0900-1400, 1700-2000. Fri. 0900-1400. Sat. 0900-1400, 2030-2300.

Castel S Angelo Lungotevere Castello. The history of the Emperor Hadrian's Mausoleum is described under *Ancient Rome*, but the *castello* also provides a unique closeup of a Roman prison, in use right up to the 19th century. Its dungeons must be among the gloomiest in the world; they inspired Piranesi's famous series of 'Prisons' etchings. You enter by the original tomb entrance and penetrate into the heart of the former imperial mausoleum along a vaulted gallery once covered with mosaics and frescoes. Among the inmates of the dungeons was the silversmith, artist and diarist Benvenuto Cellini. The collection of arms and armour is one of the best in Italy – the portable arms on show date back to the 7th century BC and include some rare Medieval weapons. Note also the stone projectiles, catapults and cannon balls used in medieval siege warfare. The elegant Papal apartment above the prison could not be in greater contrast. Pope Paul III's bedroom has been restored and decorated with furniture and porcelain of the period. The spacious Renaissance rooms were partly decorated by Perin del Vaga. The views over Rome and the Vatican from the loggia and the terrace above are stunning. Some rooms are shut owing to staff shortages and restoration work which is continuing. Models of the *castello* during different periods of its history are on show near the entrance.   **3D4**

Civilta Romana Piazzale Giovanni Agnelli, EUR. The long journey out to EUR is worth while in order to see the best scale model in Italy (scale 1:250) of ancient Rome which covers over 200 square yards (see p.80). The museum also contains numerous interesting plaster casts and models of Roman buildings from all over the Empire.
Sun. 0900-1300. Mon. closed. Tues.-Sat. 0900-1400. Metropolitana Magliana, journey time from Termini 20 minutes. The museum is a short walk up the hill from the metro station.

Museo del Folklore Romano Piazza S. Egidio, Trastevere. This newly established museum contains some fascinating dioramas illustrating various scenes of Roman daily life in the 18th – 19th centuries, including the Tavern, the Church, the Wineshop, and the Apothecary. You can still witness similar scenes here in Trastevere, a quarter which has not yet lost its village atmosphere. The collection of prints, sketches, paintings and drawings of carnival scenes, horse racing, firework displays and rare early photographs is being gradually expanded.   **6D6**
Mon. Wed. Sat. 0900-1300. Tues. Thurs. 1700-1930. Sun. 0900-1230. Closed Fri.

Keats-Shelley 26, Piazza di Spagna. The little house at the bottom right-hand corner of the Spanish Steps still retains the period charm that Keats must have sensed when he took lodgings there at the beginning of the 19th century. Now times have changed and artists and writers prefer older, cheaper quarters of the city such as Trastevere. The house, which has a good small reference library, was opened in 1909 as a memorial to both English Romantic poets who died in Italy. The then King of Italy, the President of the United States and many prominent public figures in the English speaking world supported the project with contributions. Keats' bedroom where he died on 23 February 1821 contains a death mask. He smiles in tranquillity, despite the agony of the last few weeks of his life.   **1F4**
Mon.-Fri 0900-1230, 1430-1700. Sat. Sun. closed. Entrance fee. Metropolitana Spagna

Nazionale Romano Viale delle Terme. Unlike the other main collections of Roman antique art this is not a personal selection, but the last resting place of all important ancient art works in the city, many of which needless to say are not on display but hidden away in dusty storage rooms. The museum does, however, include the splendid Ludovisi family collection begun in the 17th century and acquired in 1906, plus the largest collection of pagan and Christian sarcophagi in the world. The crown of the Ludovisi collection is the famous 'throne' discovered in 1887. A Greek work dating from the 5th century BC it most likely comes from Sicily. Aphrodite, Goddess of Love, and protectress of sailors is sculpted rising wet from the waves – a vivid portrayal of this ancient and beautiful legend. Among the many other masterpieces I would single out three: a Greek statue from the Gardens of Sallust representing a *Daughter of Niobe* trying to remove from her back an arrow shot at her by Artemis; the so-called *Girl of Anzio*, washed up on the beach after a storm near the Imperial villa at Anzio, south of Rome, in 1878, and the Lancellotti *Discus Thrower*, the best preserved Roman copy of the lost Greek original. In Hall VI do not miss a fine mosaic depicting some of the most famous 4th-century Roman charioteers. One champion called Aeri wears the palm of victory and one of his four chariot horses, Itala, is actually named by the artist. Itala must have been as famous as any modern Derby winner. Finally two unique pieces of Roman interior decoration. First, a complete frescoed garden-room from the villa of the Empress Livia discovered in the last century in a Rome suburb and brought here in the 1950s to avoid deterioration through damp. The freshness of the frescoes of trees, plants, flowers, songbirds and butterflies and the garden trellis work makes it difficult to believe that it was all painted 2000 years ago. The other Roman villa paintings, in a rather more formal style, come from a villa discovered in the Farnesina Gardens, on the banks of the

Tiber in 1879 when the river embankment was being rebuilt.   **4H4**

Tues-Sat. 0830-1400. Sun. 0900-1300. Closed Mon. Metropolitana Repubblica

Nazionale di Villa Giulia Via delle Belle Arti. The villa was the dreamhouse of the last of the Renaissance Popes, Julius III. Giorgio Vasari, better known as art historian, helped in the design of the building which was completed in 1553. The museum was founded in 1889 to bring together all the pre-Roman antiquities dug up in the provinces of Lazio, Etruria and Umbria. It is the finest of all museums devoted to the Etruscans, that mysterious people whose civilization, undeciphered language and mythology had so great an influence on the Romans, but whose origins remain obscure. The display is admirably set out, which cannot be said about many museums in Rome. The different rooms show the variety of objects recovered during over 150 years of archaeological digs. Like the Egyptians, the Etruscans buried their dead surrounded by everything they might need in the after life, including utensils for food and drink, weapons, clothing, jewellery and furniture. The *pièce de résistance* of the museum is the terra cotta sculpture from the temple in the Etruscan city of Veii, which now lies on the edge of Rome's northern suburbs. The *Apollo* and the *Hercules* are Greek in inspiration but unmistakably Etruscan in spirit. They are objects of outstanding beauty which speak to us across the centuries. They are most likely the work of an Etruscan sculptor called Velca who was commissioned to make the statues for the prestigious Temple of Jupiter on the Capitol Hill some time towards the end of the 6th century BC. Another fine example of terra cotta is the famous sarcophagus of the 'Bride and Bridegroom' from Cerveteri. The couple recline together, the man's hand lying protectively on his wife's shoulder. We know nothing at all about them except that the quality of the portraiture shows a delicacy of touch that is conspicuously lacking in later Roman tomb portraits. The Etruscans traded extensively with the Greeks, as is obvious from the huge number of Greek pots and vases dug up in Etruria. But they also produced their own distinctive black pottery called 'Bucchero' and you can still pick up sherds which litter the countryside around the sites of ancient Etruscan cities. There is some fine gold and ivory treasure to see if the Sala degli Ori happens to be open. Upstairs are some remarkable vases, plates and toilet articles, and a collection of small bronze figurines which might be the envy of many modern art museums.   **1E3**

Tues-Sat 0900-1400. Sun. 0900-1300. Closed Mon., public holidays. Metropolitana Flaminia, then a short walk or bus ride (1, 2, 90, 95) up the Via Flaminia to the narrow Via di Villa Giulia.

Museo di Palazzo Venezia Piazza Venezia and Via del Plebiscito. The first great Renaissance palace of Rome was built between 1455 and 1500 and for part of that time was the main residence of Pope Paul II, one of the great art collectors of his day. We know from contemporary descriptions that the palace was hung with tapestries and brocades and filled with gold and silver and objets d'art, most of it looted during subsequent sacks of the city. The palace marks the transition from the medieval concept of a fortress-residence to the architecturally more elegant show-palace of the Renaissance. The museum is appropriately devoted to the arts and crafts of Medieval and Renaissance Rome. The Papal apartment with its famous Sala del Mappamondo, used by Mussolini as his office during the heyday of Fascism, has been restored and refurnished in its original style. The splendid garden-courtyard is through the arch beside the Basilica of S. Marco.   **4E5**

Tues-Sat. 0900-1400. Sun. and public holidays 0900-1300. Closed Mon.

Museo Centrale del Risorgimento Via S. Pietro in Carcere. Situated beside the Victor Emmanuel Monument this is a copious collection of historical archive material. It covers the period of the Napoleonic occupation, the Roman Republic of 1849, and the unification of Italy.   **4F6**

Wed. Fri. Sun. 1000-1300 only.

Etruscan bride and bridegroom

Museo di Roma (Palazzo Braschi) 10, Piazza S. Pantaleo. Rome's municipal museum is devoted to pictures and souvenirs of Roman life during the past 400 years. It includes such curiosities as Pope Pius IX's private railway carriage used for visiting his earthly realms, costumes of the 18th century and scenes of boisterous Roman carnival celebrations. There is a rich print and photographic collection on the top floor, a useful source of research material for sociologists and historians.   **3D5**

Tues-Sat. 0900-1300. Sun. 1000-1230. Closed Mon.

Galleries

Galleria Barberini (Galleria Nazionale d'Arte Antica) Via Quattro Fontane Rome's 'National Gallery' is a mere shadow of what it ought to be. Out of the 3000 paintings in the collection, only one tenth are actually on show, including the incomparable *La Fornarina*, Raphael's portrait of his mistress, the baker's daughter Margherita. The reason is that a military officers' club leases half the available space on the piano nobile and the military refuse to budge despite protests from Italian art lovers and foreign tourists. Among the most interesting treasures of this state picture collection are an *Annunciation* by Fra Angelico, a portrait of Henry VIII of England by Hans Holbein, in which the King is depicted dressed for his wedding to his fourth wife Ann of Cleves, a *Venus and Adonis* by Titian, two fine El Grecos, and a collection of 18th-century French paintings bequeathed in 1960. The magnificent ceiling of the Great Hall of the Barberini Palace was painted by Pietro da Cortona in 1638 and its subject is the Triumph of Divine Providence, a pictorial celebration of the pontificate of the Barberini Pope Urban VIII.   **4G4**

Tues-Sat. 0900-1600. Sun. and public holidays 0900-1300. Closed Mon. Metropolitana Barberini

Borghese Piazzale del Museo Borghese. The nephew of Pope Paul V, Cardinal Scipio Borghese, built this intimate villa, originally called a *casino*, at the beginning of the 17th century and it forms the perfect backdrop for the display of his private art collection. The gardens were landscaped by a Scottish artist, Jacob More, in 1773. Napoleon forced the Prince Borghese of his day to sell over 200 pieces from the family collection to the Louvre, where they remain today. But Canova's master portrait of Napoleon's sister Pauline, who

Pauline Borghese *Canova*

married the Prince, posing semi-naked on a chaise-longue may be some slight compensation to the visitor today. In the main entrance hall you can see some vivid mosaic scenes of gladiator fights, originally dug up on one of the Borghese estates outside Rome. The gladiators marked with the Greek capital letter theta Θ (the first letter of 'thanatos' the Greek word for death) were condemned to die by thumbs down signs from the jeering crowd after losing in combat. The ground floor is devoted to sculpture, while the upper floor houses the picture gallery. In the next room to Canova's *Pauline*, is Bernini's *David*. This youthful work of the great 17th-century sculptor and architect was commissioned by the Cardinal and is one of the earliest examples of the full-blooded style later to be classified as Baroque. Upstairs are untold treasures; three Raphaels, a Botticelli, a superb self-portrait by Lorenzo Lotto, Caravaggio's *Madonna of the Palafrenieri*, Correggio's *Danae* and Titian's *Sacred and Profane Love*, one of the most mysterious allegorical paintings in the whole of Italian art.   **1G3**

Tues-Sat. 0900-1400. Sun. and public holidays 0900-1300. Closed Mon. Metropolitana Spagna. Walk through the tunnel to the underground car park in the Villa Borghese. The gallery is a ten-minute walk through the park.

Colonna 17 Via della Pilotta. Another interesting Roman private collection of paintings is to be seen in the huge Palazzo Colonna founded by the 15th-century Colonna Pope Martin V and rebuilt 300 years later. The gems of the collection are a series of Roman landscapes by Gaspare Dughet, and a Paolo Veronese portrait of an unknown nobleman. There are also some historic family portraits including that of Michelangelo's friend Vittoria Colonna, and of Marie Mancini, a 17th-century Colonna Princess who was Louis XIV's first love.   **4F5**

Sat. only 0900-1300. Closed August.

Galleria Doria-Pamphilj la, Piazza del Collegio Romano. The greatest treasure of this private picture gallery in the Palazzo Doria, one of the great princely houses of Rome, now let off into over 200 flats, is the Velasquez portrait of the Pamphilj Pope, Innocent X. Entering the gallery you enter a long vanished world of the 17th century complete with original furnishings and tapestries. Do not fail to visit the state apartments if they are open. Three Caravaggios, a *Mary Magdalene*, *Rest during the flight into Egypt* and *St John Baptist* are of exceptional interest, while you can also see five classical landscapes by Claude Lorrain and a fine series of Flemish and Roman landscapes.   **4E5**

Tues. Fri.-Sun. only 1000-1300. Bus 64. A short walk up the Via del Corso from the Piazza Venezia. Take the Via Lata on the left at the side of the Banco di Roma to get into Piazza del Collegio Romano.

Nazionale d'Arte Moderna 135, Viale delle Belle Arti. The most important collection in Italy of paintings and sculpture by 19th and 20th-century native artists forms a useful yardstick for comparison with the achievements of earlier periods.   **1F3**

Tues-Sat. 0900-1400. Sun. and public holidays 0900-1300. Closed Mon. Metro Flaminia.

Spada Piazza Capodiferro This is one of the smallest, yet most evocative, family picture collections in Rome. It was begun by Cardinal Bernardino Spada in the early years of the 17th century and is contained in only four rooms. The Cardinal himself is the subject of portraits by his friends Guido Reni, and Il Guercino. There is also an unfinished Titian, a *Visitation* by Andrea del Sarto and a Rubens portrait. The original setting is accurately preserved. In the garden of the Palazzo do not fail to inspect the trompe l'oeil perspective of a gallery designed by Borromini. It is a fine piece of Baroque sleight-of-hand. The 'gallery' with the statue at the end is an optical illusion, it is only ten yards long. The Palazzo itself is now occupied by Italy's highest judicial tribunal, the Consiglio di Stato, whose special written permission is required to·visit the State apartments. The Sala del Baldacchino (throne room) is a reminder that princely families in Rome used to keep a special room available for a visit by the Pope. The room contains an antique statue long believed (most likely in

error according to modern research) to have been the famous statue of Pompey at whose feet Julius Caesar was murdered in the Capitol.   **3D5**

Tues-Sat. 0900-1400 Sun. and public holidays 0900-1300. Closed Mon.

Villa della Farnesina Via della Lungara, Trastevere. This graceful Renaissance villa on the banks of the Tiber was built by Baldassare Peruzzi for the Sienese Banker Agostino Chigi. The villa was decorated by Raphael and his pupils, including Giulio Romano, Savastiano del Piombo, and Sodoma. Chigi's legendary banquets attended by the Pope, Cardinals, eminent diplomats and men of letters, often ended up riotously with the guests throwing the gold plate off which they had eaten into the river. But their host had artfully arranged an underwater net to recover his treasure after the meal. You now enter by what used to be the back door. Proceed directly to the former main entrance, the Gallery, which has a painted ceiling designed by Raphael depicting the story of Psyche. The loggia is now glassed in, but was originally designed to give access directly to the garden. In the room next door, is a fresco composition actually executed by Raphael's own hand, the famous Galatea. This loggia was also originally designed to open on to the garden. Upstairs is the great living room of the villa known as the Sala delle Prospettive (Hall of Perspectives). There are fascinating details of 16th-century Rome hidden among Baldassare Peruzzi's trompe l'oeil painting. Next door is Agostino's bedroom frescoed by Sodoma with scenes from the life of Alexander the Great and recently restored. The villa was bought towards the end of the 16th century by the Farnese family which accounts for its present name. On the top floor is the *Gabinetto Nazionale delle Stampe* a library of old prints which is frequently used for temporary exhibitions of old master prints and drawings from its extensive and valuable collection.   **3D5**

Open Tues-Sat. and Sun. 1000-1200 Closed Mon.

Vatican Museums

The entrance is in Viale Vaticano near Piazza Risorgimento. There is also a regular free bus service from Piazza S.Pietro (on the left of Bernini's Colonnades as you face the Basilica). The Vatican houses one of the world's great art collections. Its 7km/4½mi of exhibits will daunt even the most energetic tourist. So if you only have limited time plan to take in what interests you most – and hurry past the rest. A one-way system operates for security reasons, so work out in advance what you wish to miss – you cannot go back for example to the **Stanze di Rafaello** *after* visiting the **Capella Sistina** (Sistine Chapel). Remember also that the Sistine chapel is a long walk – about 400m/¼mi from the entrance along many corridors and staircases.

Popes have been collecting antique art for at least 500 years and today the Vatican contains the largest number of Greek and Roman statues, reliefs, mosaics and inscriptions of any museum in the world. The **Museo Pio Clementino** takes its name from two 18th-century Popes who tried to put some order among the large number of pieces of classical statuary littering the Vatican gardens and palaces. Note the splendid 4th-century porphyry sarcophagi in the **Sala a Croce Greca** (hall in the shape of a Greek cross), also a sculpted head (no.567) that is most likely a portrait of Cleopatra.

Laöcoon

In the octagonal courtyard of the **Belvedere Palace**, which was the creation of one of the main founders of the Vatican collection, Pope Julius II, you can see one of the most famous sculptures of ancient Greece, the *Laocoön*, a marble group of the 2nd century BC dug up on the Esquiline hill in 1506. Laocoön, a priest of Apollo, and his sons were suffocated by serpents as a punishment by the gods. Opposite is the *Apollo del Belvedere* a fine Roman copy of a famous 4th-century BC Greek bronze.

Nearby in the **Atrio del Torso** is the famous *Torso del Belvedere* a fragment of a naked figure seated on the skin of a wild animal. The hidden power in this much damaged piece of marble is reputed to have impressed even Michelangelo.

The **Braccio Nuovo** (New Wing) a 19th-century addition, contains a telling portrait of Augustus (No.14) at about the age of 40, and a colossal statue of the Nile river god surrounded by sphinxes and crocodiles.

You now penetrate into part of the **Vatican Library**. In the **Sala Sistina** is a strange wooden device which was used to fix the Papal seal or 'bollo' on important Papal documents or 'Bulls' as they were called in English. The central reading room is laid out with various valuable codices, or handwritten versions of the Bible, some written on papyrus. The Library contains over 70,000 codices, manuscripts and early printed books. On display are a set of love letters from King Henry VIII to Ann Boleyn (evidence used against the sovereign in excommunication proceedings), an illustrated book on falconry by the Holy Roman Emperor Frederick II, and autograph letters of Michelangelo and Raphael.

The **Capella Sistina** is perhaps the most famous and overwhelming of all Rome's art treasures. The chapel, built by Pope Sixtus IV at the end of the 15th century, was decorated by some of the greatest artists of the day, including Botticelli, Signorelli, and Pinturicchio. But it was Michelangelo's painting of the huge ceiling between 1508 and 1512 and his masterpiece, the *Last Judgement* painted on the main altar wall 23 years later that set the seal of greatness on the building. Michelangelo was at first reluctant to carry out Pope Julius II's commission to paint the events of the Creation, and had the greatest difficulty in getting paid for his *tour de force*. Refusing all assistance, he locked himself away for years, lying on his back suspended from scaffolding in order to cover with paint over 3000sq m/10,000 sq ft of ceiling. It is a feat that still takes away the breath of the steady stream of visitors who pass through the chapel every day.

If the Creation breathes the very spirit of the Renaissance at its height, the *Last Judgement* is in very different mood. *Terribilità* (terribleness) was the quality in Michelangelo's art that most impressed his contemporaries, and here with Christ standing in final judgement over humanity (including many actual portraits of the artist's friends and enemies), you feel Michelangelo is making his final statement on life and death,

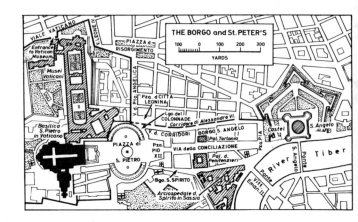

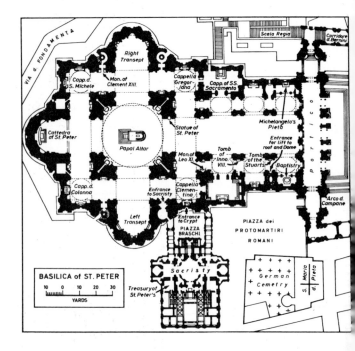

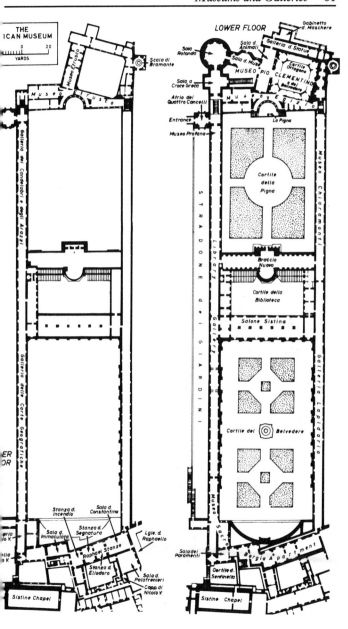

THE
ICAN MUSEUM

0   20
YARDS

Scala di
Bramante

Museo Etrusco

M U S E O   E T R U S C O

Galleria dei Candelabri e degli Arazzi

Galleria delle Carte Geografiche

ER
OR

Stanza d.
Incendio

Sala d.
Constantine

Sala d.
Immaculata

Stanza d.
Segnatura

Lgie. d.
Raphaello

Raphael Stanze

eria
lo V.

Stanza d.
Eliodoro

Sala d.
Palafrenieri

lla
o V.

Capp. di
Nicolo V.

Sistine Chapel

LOWER FLOOR

Gabinetto
d. Maschere

Sala
Rotonda

Sala d.
Animali

Galleria d. Statue

Sala d. Muse

Cortile
Ottagono

MUSEO PIO

CLEMENTINO
e del Belvedere

Sala a
Croce Greca

M U S E O   P I O   C L E M E N T I N O

Atrio dei
Quattro Cancelli

Entrance

Museo Profano

La Pigna

Cortile
della
Pigna

Braccio
Nuovo

Cortile della
Biblioteca

Salone Sistina

Cortile del   Belvedere

Sala dei
Paramenti

Cortile d.
Sentinella

Sistine Chapel

ergia Apartment

S T R A D O N E   d e i   G I A R D I N I

L i b r a r y   G a l l e r y

Museo Sacro

Museo Chiaramonti

Galleria Lapidaria

honour and ambition, love and hate. The *Last Judgement* did not meet with universal approval. Prudish Popes ordered trousers or loin cloths to be painted on some of the nudes. (They were later removed.) The Sistine Chapel is today used for the election of a new Pope on the death of the Roman Pontiff, and for solemn assemblies of the College of Cardinals.

While Michelangelo was labouring alone on his great ceiling, his rival and fellow artist Raphael was working (with plenty of assistants) on the decoration of the nearby **Stanze di Rafaello**. (Raphael Rooms). This was the private apartment of Pope Julius II who did not want to live in the **Borgia Apartment** below, because of its unpleasant historical associations. Two of the rooms, the **Stanza della Segnatura**, the Pope's study and library, and the **Stanza di Eliodoro**, his bedroom, are mostly by Raphael's own hand. Truth, beauty and goodness are the subjects of the frescoes in the first room. The *Disputation of the Sacrament* and the *School of Athens* represent respectively religious and philosophical truth, while Apollo and the Muses on Mount Parnassus represent beauty. Goodness is portrayed by the cardinal virtues, prudence, temperance and strength. The second room contains three superb frescoes; the *Expulsion of Heliodorus from the Temple in Jerusalem*, *Pope Leo Stopping the Invasion of Attila the Hun*, and the *Miracle of Bolsena*.

The **Museo Gregoriano Etrusco** should not be missed as it contains the Etruscan treasure discovered in 1837 in a tomb at Cerveteri (then part of the Pope's earthly domain). The three occupants of the tomb were buried with gold, silver, jewels, and richly decorated table ware. The **Museo Profano** and the **Museo Cristiano** (Profane and Christian Museums) used to be housed in the Lateran Palace and were transferred here into a new building in 1970. They contain Roman sculpture, inscriptions and sarcophagi dating from the 1st-4th centuries AD. The 4th-century statue of the Good Shepherd is an excellent example of the continuity of Mediterranean art forms – the inspiration is clearly pagan and ancient Greek.

If you are not too exhausted, the **Pinacoteca** or Vatican Picture Gallery contains further riches. It is particularly well endowed with Primitives and 13th-century Italian artists. The Giotto polyptych in Room II and the Melozzo da Forlì Angels in Room IV are worth more than a passing glance. In Room VIII there is a Raphael feast. The *Transfiguration*, Raphael's last work (it was hung above his bier as he lay in state) has been cleaned recently, revealing unexpected new details. Also on view is a set of tapestries woven from Raphael's cartoons for the Capella Sistina, now in the Victoria and Albert Museum in London. The *Coronation of the Virgin* was the first work of Raphael's maturity – he was 20 years old when he painted it.

Open Mon.-Sat. 0900–1400 Closed Sun. and all religious holidays (except last Sunday in each Month when the Museums are open and admission is free). At Easter and from July-Sep opening times are normally extended until 1700 daily. Snackbar available for refreshments and light lunches. Wheelchairs available for disabled upon prior application.

Hercules

Vatican Gardens

A surprising oasis of tranquility with well-manicured lawns watered by automatic sprinklers lies behind St Peter's Basilica. Guided tours of the Pope's gardens take place three times a week (see Vatican City). You begin the tour near the Railway Station where once a week a duty free goods wagon is still shunted in on a branch line but no passenger trains run. The medieval tower of S.Giovanni has been converted into a residence for official Vatican guests. Passing alongside a replica of the Grotto at Lourdes, you come to

Vatican Radio, where Marconi himself first set up transmissions for the Holy See in 1931. A shady wood, a Rose Garden, several fountains and the Vatican Mint complete the tour.

Vatican Gardens

MONUMENTS

Colonna Antonina 4E5

Piazza Colonna The Antoninus column, better known as Marcus Aurelius' column, which dominates the hub of central Rome was erected in 28 monolitti blocks around AD 180 to commemorate the victory of the Emperor Marcus Aurelius over the tribes then inhabiting Germany. The vivid bas reliefs in spiral around the column were restored in the 16th century and are now suffering severe erosion due to atmospheric pollution. A spiral staircase of 190 steps leads to the top where Domenico Fontana replaced the original statue of Marcus Aurelius with one of St Paul in 1588.

Colonna Traiana 4F5

Foro di Traiano (See also Foro di Traiano) Perhaps the finest of ancient Roman triumphal columns, Trajan's Column (AD 113) in its spiral frieze is a lively record of the main events in the military campaign by the Emperor Trajan against the Dacians (a tribe living in the territory now known as Romania) at the beginning of the 2nd century AD. There are more than 2500 figures in the marble bas relief, originally painted in full colour. Alas, today many of them are seriously damaged by atmospheric pollution. The Emperor's statue that stood on the top of the column was replaced in 1587 by that of St Peter's. Trajan's ashes were once kept in a golden urn in the base of the monument.

Monumento a Giuseppe Garibaldi 6C6

Piazzale del Gianicolo Giuseppe Garibaldi (1807–82) was the soldier-hero of modern Italy. He fought against the French during the short-lived Roman Republic in 1849. The decisive battle took place here on the Gianicolo and when the modern Italian state was founded in 1870, the hill was laid out as a park. The equestrian statue of Garibaldi dates from 1895. The hero turns his head defiantly towards the Vatican. The terrace in front of the monument provides one of the finest panoramas of Rome. Any bus the Gianicolo

Monumento a Vittorio Emanuele 4F5

Piazza Venezia This monumental eyesore of white Brescian marble in the centre of Rome was built to celebrate the unification of Italy and completed in 1911. The Altare della Patria, on the first level contains the tomb of Italy's unknown soldier, added after the First World War, and is the equivalent of the Cenotaph in London. The monument is so out of scale with the architectural treasures which surround it that all comment is superfluous. It has been christened variously as the 'wedding cake' or the 'typewriter'. At the side is the **Museo Nazionale del Risorgimento** (see p.56) which will be of interest to students of modern Italian history. Bus 64 Piazza Venezia.

Statue Parlanti

(Speaking statues) For centuries a series of ancient Roman statues, given names such as Madama Lucrezia, Marforio and Pasquino, have fulfilled a very Roman role in political satire, particularly against the Pope. Epigrams and simple graffiti were copied onto cards which were hung around the necks of the various busts. The most famous of these statues, a bust of Menelaus, known as Pasquino, is in the Piazza Pasquino, off the Via S. Maria dell' Anima. In 1870 the famous abbreviation SPQR, *Senatus Populusque Romanus*, the Senate and the people of Rome, which now adorns the works of the contemporary municipality such as drain covers, streetlamps and buses, was said by Pasquino to mean *Sanctus Pater Quondam Rex*, The Holy Father Once a King, after the loss of the Pope's temporal power when Italy was united.

Trajan's Column and Victor Emmanuel Monument

Stairway to the Capitol

Dioscuri 4F5

(Castor and Pollux) *Piazza del Quirinale*
The gigantic statues of the mythological
horse tamers Castor and Pollux are Roman copies of Greek originals. The
names of Phidias and Praxiteles sculpted on the base are mere wishful think-
ing on the part of Sixtus V who moved
them here. The original statues probably adorned the Baths of Constantine
and the marble basin was brought from
the Foro Romano where for centuries it
fulfilled a useful purpose as a cattle
trough.

Marcus Aurelius 4F5

Piazza del Campidoglio This equestrian
statue is one of the greatest single
bronzes to have survived from antiquity
and escaped being melted down during
the Middle Ages due to a mistake. For
centuries the bronze was believed to
represent Constantine, the first Christian Emperor. The bronze was taken to
the Campidoglio in 1583 to adorn
Michelangelo's palazzo and he designed
the plinth of the statue. Some of the
original gilding which once covered the
bronze can still be seen on the head and
flanks of the horse. Recent studies show
that the bronze has suffered severe cor-
rosion from atmospheric pollution. The
authorities intend to remove the statue
to the nearby museum and replace it in
the piazza with a replica as has been
done in Venice with the famous antique
bronze horses of St Mark's also removed from their original site for better
conservation.

Bus 64 – Piazza Venezia.

Marcus Aurelius

TOURS ON FOOT

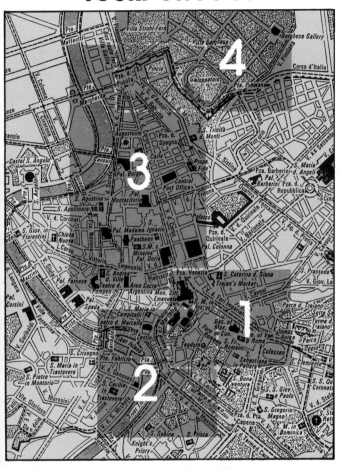

1 Ancient Rome 2.2km/1⅜mi
This walk takes you through what could be called the cradle of western civilization. This small area was the hub of the Roman empire.

2 Roman Churches 2.2km/1⅜mi
There are more than 1000 churches in Rome and this tour will give you some idea of the architectural diversity in one small area straddling the Tiber.

3 Central Rome 2.4km/1½mi
Architectural and artistic triumphs abound in this part of Rome. This walk takes you to some of these and leads to the splendour of the Piazza Navona.

4 Museums in the Park 1.6km/1mi
This short walk through the park between two beautiful museums can last as long as you like depending on your interest in the museums and enjoyment of the park.

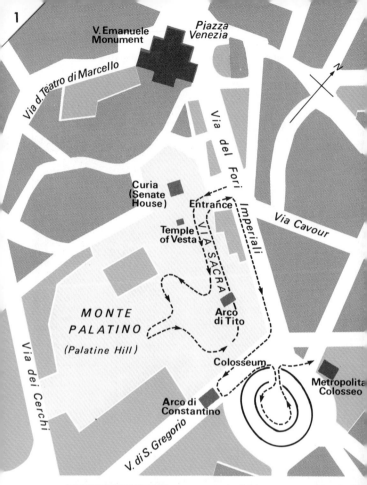

1

ANCIENT ROME

Rome had its beginnings in the area known for centuries as the **Foro Romano** (Roman Forum) and the **Palatino** (Palatine Hill) and a morning wandering around one of the world's most evocative archaeological sites is an essential part of any stay in Rome, however long or short the time at your disposal. Within a relatively small area lie the remains of the centres of government, religion and entertainment of the ancient city – the Senate House, the Temple of Vesta, and the Colosseum. It was while wandering here one October morning in 1764 that Edward Gibbon conceived his monumental work *The Decline and Fall of the Roman Empire*.

Begin the tour at the main entrance to the Forum in the Via dei Fori Imperiali (entrance fee). You walk straight into the Via Sacra (Sacred Way), the original paved Roman road which was the hub of the ancient city. On your right stands the imposing square redbrick Curia (Senate House). Although rebuilt many times, the last occasion being the reign of the 3rd-century Emperor Diocletian, this was the Roman people's Assembly to which every modern parliament owes its origin. The building was preserved because for centuries until its last restoration in the 1930s it was in use as a church.

Amid the truncated temple columns and ruined walls look now for the remains of the graceful white marble Temple of Vesta, built in AD 191 under the reign of the Emperor Septimius Severus, whose large triumphal arch dominates this part of the Forum. The Vestal Virgins, who lived in an adjacent house were the guardians of a sacred flame that burnt in perpetuity on the altar of the goddess and symbolized the continuity of the Roman State. The white-robed Vestals, who were recruited for their prestigious position between the ages of six and ten, survived as a sorority performing their pagan rites well into the Christian era.

The Arch of Titus at the south end of the Forum was erected by the Emperor Titus to celebrate his capture of Jerusalem in AD 70. The relief on the inside of the arch shows loot, including the seven branched candelabra, being hauled away from the Temple by the victorious Romans.

Walk up the steps bearing slightly to the right and you will come to the formal gardens on the Palatino, one of the seven hills of the ancient city, and in turn prehistoric fortress, chic residential area and imperial palace. The pleasure gardens were laid out by a Farnese Cardinal in the 16th century. The Palatino is a honeycomb of ruined palaces and houses almost impossible for the layman to identify as you pick your way through the crumbling remains. Here perhaps better than anywhere else in the city you can capture the colours and atmosphere which inspired generations of landscape painters from all over Europe to try to put it all down on canvas. The rich marble decorations, the sumptuous imperial palaces are no

more – they have long been destroyed and looted – but you can still gain an impression of the interior of a Roman house in the early days of the Empire from the **Casa di Livia** (House of Livia) with some of its original frescoes of mythological scenes and festoons of fruit and flowers. This was the domestic décor of wealthy patrician families in the century before Christ's birth. The Emperor Augustus was born in a house here on the Palatino in 63 BC.

Retrace your steps to the entrance to the Forum, and turn right down the Via dei Fori Imperiali towards the **Colosseo** (Colosseum). The four-storied amphitheatre is above all an architectural tour de force. The elliptical building measures over 530m/580yd in circumference and could hold over 50,000 spectators. For three hundred years it was the scene of gladiatorial combats of extreme ferocity and cruelty, mock naval battles, and public massacres in which criminals and other undesireables such as Christians, were fed to wild beasts. The Colosseo has been pillaged for centuries as a quarry for building other Roman monuments and palaces. The holes on the outside of the façade were caused by the removal during the Middle Ages of metal cramps used to hold the stones together. The newly opened small museum of gladiator-lore is worth a visit.

The nearby **Arco di Costantino** (Arch of Constantine) was erected in AD 315 to celebrate the victory of the first Christian Emperor of Rome at the Ponte Milvio (Milvian Bridge) in the north of the city. The reliefs are distinctly pagan in character, but do not be surprised; the Arch was erected well before the Emperor's final conversion.

Forum, from the Capitol

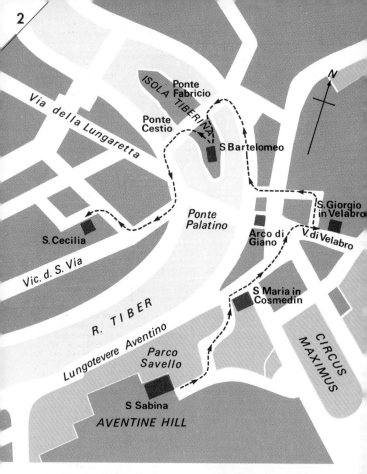

2

ROMAN CHURCHES

The tour begins on the Aventine Hill at the church of **S. Sabina**, one of the most perfect early Christian basilicas in Rome, skilfully restored in the 1930s. The golden sunlight pouring through the translucent alabaster windows in the morning hours is unforgettable. The church was built in the middle of the 5th century AD on the site of a house belonging to a Roman lady called Sabina. The matched white marble Corinthian columns most likely came from the palace of a pagan Emperor. It is unusual to find such harmony and uncluttered simplicity in Roman churches which have often been overlaid by cen-

S. Sabina

turies of embellishment reflecting changing styles and architectural tastes

The gold and blue mosaic dedicatory inscription above the main door was made in the 5th century while the unusual windows and the carved choir date from the 9th century.

Turn left as you leave the church and spend five minutes in the **Parco Savello**, a walled public garden full of orange trees with a fine view over the Tiber and the city. Bearing left again and continuing down the narrow Clivo di Monte Savello, you walk down to the river. Turn right along the Via S. Maria in Cosmedin and you will see the campanile of the church of the same name on your right.

In the portico of the church you can see the famous **Bocca della Verità** (Mouth of Truth) a huge stone draincover dating from classical times and representing the face of a river god. In medieval times the Bocca was in use as a sort of primitive lie-detector. The mask was said to snap off the fingers of anyone who had told a lie who inserted their hand inside its open mouth.

S. Maria in Cosmedin was built over the ruins of the ancient city's main food distribution office, and some columns from this important building are incorporated into the nave of the church. Observe the floor – it is a fine example of the mosaics produced by the Cosmati, a group of Roman decorators who worked in the 12th and 13th centuries and who produced fine geometrical designs with combinations of large and small triangles, squares and circles of coloured marble.

Outside again continue into the Via del Velabro where you cannot miss the **Arco di Giano** (Arch of Janus) dating probably from the 4th century. This was a busy commercial centre in the ancient city and the arch provided shade and shelter from the elements for merchants and their customers.

A few yards away lies the romanesque church of **S. Giorgio in Velabro**. This is a good example of how the building materials of Rome were used and used again. The sixteen columns which divide the triple nave, originally belonged to ancient Roman temples and were salvaged for the construction of the original church in the 6th century. It is a popular church for weddings.

Next door is an ancient Roman relic – the **Arco degli Argentari** (Arch of the Moneychangers) dating from the reign of the 2nd-century Emperor Septimius Severus. In front of the arch you can trace the remains of the **Cloaca Maxima** (Great Sewer) which carried the sewage and floodwater of the ancient city into the Tiber. You can still see the exit of the sewer into the river near the ruined Ponte Rotto (Broken Bridge) about 200m/200yd upstream.

Following the river bank now past the graceful circular **Tempio di Vesta** (Temple of Vesta) you will come to the Isola Tiberina (Island in the Tiber). Crossing by the Ponte Fabricio, the oldest surviving river bridge in Rome, which dates back to 62 BC, visit the exquisitely restored church of **S. Bartolomeo**.

The island used to be the centre of the cult of the Greek god of medicine, Aesculapius. His temple attracted sufferers from many diseases who often brought with them a small terracotta model of the part of the body to be cured. Hundreds of these *ex voto* arms, legs or heads have been dug up on the island by archaeologists. Inside S. Bartolomeo you can see a well head which may mark the healing spring of Aesculapius' temple. In a side chapel to the left of the main altar are some frescoes showing the floating water-mills which used to be anchored off the island for milling grain until about a hundred years ago. Walk down some steps near the church to get down to river-level. At the extremity of the island is one of Rome's most unusual police stations – the River Police Headquarters where divers are on 24-hour alert to save anyone who is unfortunate enough to fall into what the Roman historian Tacitus accurately described as the 'yellowish' Tiber.

Continue over the river by another ancient Roman bridge, the Ponte Cestio, and you are in Trastevere, a crowded suburb in both ancient and modern Rome. The last church on our tour, **S. Cecilia**, lies behind a maze of narrow streets – don't be afraid to ask the way if you find the map difficult to follow. Romans are usually delighted to help stray tourists find their bearings.

The church of S. Cecilia is said to have been built over the house where Cecilia, the early Christian martyr lived and died. Her body was buried outside the city walls, but in the 10th century at the command of a Pope, Cecilia was brought back to Trastevere and reburied wrapped in golden robes under the high altar here.

Ask the nuns in the adjacent cloistered convent for permission to see the stunning fresco of the Last Judgement by the 13th-century artist Pietro Cavallini. It is a work of rare beauty and is the only large painting by Cavallini that is known to have survived.

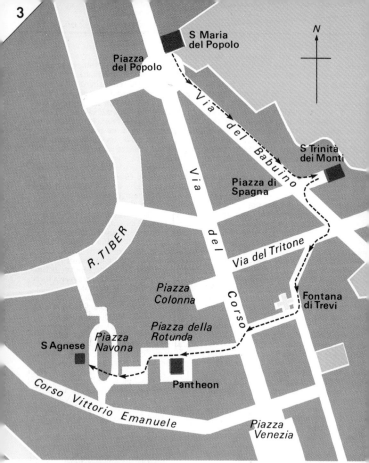

CENTRAL ROME

This walk takes you through the centre
of renaissance and medieval Rome to a
remarkable pedestrian oasis – the
Piazza Navona, site of Bernini's great
Fountain of the Rivers.

Begin at the **Piazza del Popolo**, at
the northern end of the Via del Corso.
The church of **S. Maria del Popolo** was
erected on the site of what was traditionally believed to have been the burial
place of the Roman Emperor Nero. The
church is full of remarkable treasures
(see p.87) but don't fail to see the twin
paintings by Caravaggio, the *Conversion
of St Paul* and the *Crucifixion of St
Peter*, and the Chigi family chapel designed by Raphael.

In the centre of the Piazza is a granite
obelisk originally looted from Egypt by
the Emperor Augustus, and re-erected
here by Pope Sixtus V after it had
adorned the Circus Maximus – the
racetrack of the ancient city – for centuries. The twin churches of **S. Maria
di Monte Santo** and **S. Maria dei
Miracoli** were commissioned by the
17th-century Pope Alexander VII to
form a fitting architectural conclusion
to this famous Piazza, for many hundreds of years the main entry point into
the city for all travellers arriving from
the north.

Walk down the street to the left of
the twin churches, the Via del Babuino,
to the **Piazza di Spagna**. The square got
its name from the Spanish embassy

established there in the early 17th century when the Piazza became popular as a centre for foreigners on the grand tour who found it a convenient quarter for renting rooms. The elegant **Scalinata** (Spanish Steps) leading up to the church of Trinità dei Monti was built in the 1720s and has been one of Rome's most popular tourist attractions ever since.

The English poet **John Keats** died in a lodging-house on the right hand side of the Spanish Steps on 23 February 1821. Today the house is a museum maintained by contributions from the poet's admirers all over the world. Bernini's delicate fountain **La Barcaccia** (The Barge) is almost submerged in the maelstrom of traffic that swirls around it at most hours of the day and night. Continue along the Via di Propaganda (named after the Vatican College for the Propagation of the Faith – *Propaganda Fide* in Latin – now translated as 'Evangelization' for propaganda has become a dirty word) into the Via del Tritone. Cross over into the narrow Via della Stamperia and you will soon hear the splashing of the waters of the **Fontana di Trevi** (Trevi fountain). This theatrical waterscape emerging unexpectedly in the bustling city centre is one of the most popular ports of call for the hordes of summer visitors. The cool waters of the fountain arrive via an ancient Roman aqueduct – the Acqua Vergine – but are now recycled. The Rome City Council gets the income from the coins thrown in by visitors who insist on ensuring their eventual return to the Eternal City by treating the fountain as a wishing-well.

Make now for the main north-south axis in central Rome, the Via del Corso, so called because of the popular horse races held there for centuries especially at carnival time, and cross over, continuing along any of the narrow alleys running at right angles to the Corso. Aim for the **Piazza della Rotonda** and the **Pantheon**. The Temple of all the Gods was begun in 25 BC and is the most complete and impressive ancient building to have survived in Rome. For nineteen centuries the dome of the Pantheon was the biggest in the world and its bronze doors are also the largest in existence from the ancient world.

Inside the Pantheon you can see a small segment of the original marble decoration and the tombs of the painter Raphael and the first two kings of the modern Italian State.

In the 19th century when the river Tiber used to flood regularly every winter, before the construction of its present embankment, boat trips were organized for tourists. Rowing into the Pantheon under a full moon shining through the hole in the centre of the dome was a romantic experience.

Continuing in the same general direction in which you arrived at the Pantheon, make for the **Piazza S. Eustachio** (pausing for one of the best cups of espresso coffee available in Rome at the bar of the same name if you feel in need of refreshment.) Keep going over the Corso del Rinascimento and you will find yourself in the **Piazza Navona** whose elliptical shape follows the contours of the ancient Circus Agonalis – the Emperor Domitian's athletic stadium. Today the Piazza has become the haunt of instant portrait artists, hippie tourists, drug addicts and dropouts of sundry nationalities, but an ice-cream at one of the cafes on the Piazza can still mark the perfect end to a walk through the historic centre of

Fountain of the Rivers

Rome. While you gaze at the centrepiece, the **Fontana dei Fiume** (Fountain of the Rivers), don't neglect the equally important baroque church of **S. Agnese**, the masterpiece of Borromini. Inside are his dramatic marble reliefs of the death and apotheosis of the teenage martyr Agnes. Plans are afoot to flood the Piazza Navona in summer to hold mock naval spectacles again after a lapse of several centuries.

MUSEUMS IN THE PARK

One of the most tiring aspects about a visit to Rome can be the dutiful trailing around the numerous museums and galleries usually followed by a bout of that well known tourist affliction, cultural indigestion. This tour may provide an antidote – a longish and relaxing walk between a morning visit to two of the most interesting and aesthetically pleasing museums in Rome, the Etruscan Museum at the **Villa Giulia**, essential for an understanding of the precursors of Rome, and the **Galleria Borghese** picture gallery in the **Villa Borghese Park,** an outstanding private art collection. Both museums were originally built as country villas for recreation and repose by pleasure-loving Princes of the Church, the former by Pope Julius III and the latter by Cardinal Scipio Borg-

hese, favourite nephew of Pope Paul V.

Begin the walk at the Villa Giulia, built in 1551 as a pleasure house for the Pope in what was then the countryside. The Pope filled his enormous garden with trees, exotic plants and antique statuary which in those days was still lying in abundance in and around the city.

The park has mostly been eaten up by Rome's modern concrete jungle but the Villa Giulia remains an exquisite example of a Renaissance country house, with its subtly interconnected porticoes, split level formal garden and reception rooms. The interior has been well modernized to house the most complete collection of Etruscan art anywhere in the world.

The ancient Etruscans were laid to rest surrounded by the objects of their daily life – including jewellery, kitchen ware, toilet articles, vases, statuary and weapons. The portrayal of the gods and goddesses of Etruscan mythology is of superb quality – don't miss the Apollo and Hercules from the city of Veii on the ground floor. The Etruscan bride and bridegroom lying side by side on their sarcophagus are not remote figures from a forgotten civilization, they belong to the Mediterranean world we know. Upstairs you can see writing tablets filled with the letters that later formed the basis of the Latin, and our own, alphabet. The Etruscan language remains undeciphered, but the spirit of this pre-Roman people cries out to you as you wander round this outstanding museum.

Turn right along the Via delle Belle Arti as you leave the Villa Giulia and enter the Villa Borghese park after about 300m/yds by the Viale di Valle Giulia. Now you can wander at will under the umbrella pines, past the **Piazza di Siena** where the Rome Horse Show is held every June, and you may recapture the atmosphere of the gardens of Rome before the city outgrew itself. Galleria Borghese lies at the north-east end of the park, approached along a traffic-free road, – beware of bicycles!

Cardinal Scipio Borghese's art collection proves his discernment not only for works by the established master painters of the Renaissance, such as Raphael and Titian, but also for his contemporaries including Caravaggio and the sculptor Gian Lorenzo Bernini.

The mosaic in the entrance hall – dug up from a Roman villa on one of the Borghese family estates – gives one of the most vivid pictures in Rome of the ferocity of a gladiatorial combat. Do not miss the sexy white marble statue of **Pauline Bonaparte** by Canova. Many of the best pieces of sculpture in the Cardinal's original collection were sold off to the Louvre for a song by Pauline's husband Prince Camillo Borghese. Titian's *Sacred and Profane Love* alone makes a visit to the Galleria worthwhile.

When you have exhausted the treasures of the Cardinal, walk back across the park to the Pincio Gardens for one of the classic views of Rome – including the Dome of St Peter's. For lunch try the terrace snack bar at the nearby Casina Valadier – not a very varied menu, but good cool white wine and an incomparable open-air setting in which to mull over the marvels you have been absorbing.

Pincio Terrace

Curia

Basilica of Constantine or Maxentius

Temple of Castor and Pollux

Forum, from Basilica Julia

Colosseum

Arch of Titus

Forum, from the Colosseum

Via Sacra

ANCIENT ROME

This model of ancient Rome at the time of Constantine, AD 306—37, by I. Gismondi,

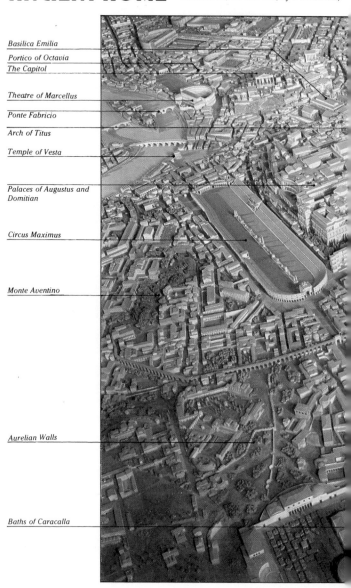

Basilica Emilia

Portico of Octavia

The Capitol

Theatre of Marcellus

Ponte Fabricio

Arch of Titus

Temple of Vesta

Palaces of Augustus and Domitian

Circus Maximus

Monte Aventino

Aurelian Walls

Baths of Caracalla

*can be seen in the Museo della Civiltà
Romana, in EUR. (See pp.55).*

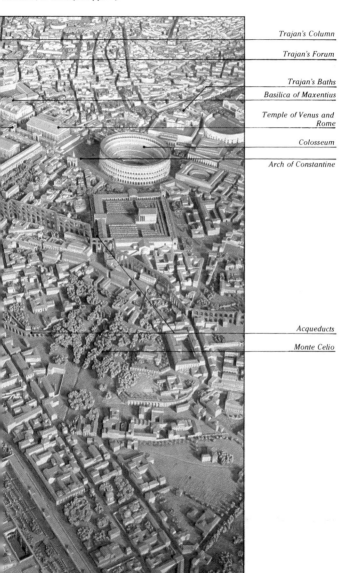

Trajan's Column

Trajan's Forum

Trajan's Baths

Basilica of Maxentius

Temple of Venus and
Rome

Colosseum

Arch of Constantine

Acqueducts

Monte Celio

Temple of Vesta, so-called, Piazza Bocca della Verita

Temple of Antoninus and Faustina, Forum

Arch of Janus, Piazza Bocca della Verita

Temple of Fortuna Virilis, Piazza Bocca della Verita

GAZETTEER

The chief monuments and architectural delights of Rome are mostly concentrated within a relatively small walkable area enclosed by the **Aurelian walls**. However, the richness of the city's historical remains and the close juxtaposition of churches, monuments and museums belonging to widely different styles and periods means that it is impossible to suggest itineraries which are going to satisfy everyone – the casual holidaymaker, the lover of romantic ruins, the specialist in baroque architecture and the devout pilgrim. For the purpose of simplicity therefore, the main places of interest in Rome are listed alphabetically by category to enable you to select most easily the places you wish to see in the time you have available.

Don't rush around trying to see everything – you cannot. And remember that Rome's charm depends on a subtle combination of season, time of day, colour, weather and mood, which means that a casual street scene, a hidden piazza or fountain can often be as arresting as the great set pieces.

Follow the map and if possible, walk. If you have come to Rome by car, park it safely having previously removed all your luggage and valuables. Don't try to master the complicated one way street and no-parking system designed to deter Romans from causing a permanent traffic jam in their city.

The buses tend to be fearfully crowded and you risk having your pocket picked as well as being squeezed to death in the rush towards the exit. The 64 double decker bus that runs through the city centre from Termini Railway Station to the Vatican is the most useful bus line. It passes along the Via Nazionale, through Piazza Venezia and Piazza Argentina and along the Corso Vittorio Emanuele. The new Metropolitana (Underground) line from the Prati area near the Vatican to S. Giovanni Laterano is only of limited use as it runs to the north of most points of interest to visitors in the city centre.

Taxis are not exhorbitantly expensive and hailing a passing yellow cab to take you back to your hotel at the end of an exhausting morning or afternoon may be the best way to end your chosen itinerary.

Each gazetteer entry bears a number identifying its general location in the city as well as a map reference. It would make sense therefore to divide your sightseeing within the city walls into the following areas: **1** Centro Storico (historic centre), **2** Foro Romano, **3** Aventino, **4** Trastevere/Isola Tiberina, **5** Quirinale/Esquilino/Celio, **6** Vatican, **7** refers to all gazetteer entries outside the Aurelian walls.

The monuments of ancient Rome are seriously threatened by atmospheric pollution. For the foreseeable future visitors to Rome are likely to be restricted in their access to and vision of the ruins which have inspired and delighted travellers for many centuries. Protective scaffolding encases many monuments and funds and expertise are lacking for an adequate conservation programme. Many structures were damaged in the earthquake which rocked the city in September 1979 and the basic problem of how to stem the accelerating deterioration of stonework without erecting ungainly shelters remains unresolved. The Via della Consolazione which cuts across the Foro Romano behind the Capitol has been closed to traffic since the earthquake owing to the danger of falling masonry. The historic Ponte Milvio, site of the battle north of the city in which the first Christian Emperor Constantine was victorious, has also been closed because of damage caused by traffic vibrations.

The main building materials used by the Romans were *tufa*, a porous volcanic stone, reddish or blackish in colour according to where it was quarried; *travertine*, a strong yellowish limestone also quarried locally; bricks, first square or diamond shaped, then flat and rectangular and marble from the Carrara quarries first exploited on a large scale by Augustus, and imported from Africa and Asia Minor. Perhaps one of the greatest Roman inventions was concrete – in the 2nd century BC. The great vaults, arches and apses of Roman architecture would have been impossible to construct without this basic building material.

1 Ara Pacis Augustae   4E4

Lungotevere in Augusta Augustus' Altar of Peace is one of the best preserved monuments of ancient Rome, thanks to the ugly but pollution-resistant shelter built during Fascist times. The altar was consecrated on 4 July 13 BC to celebrate *Pax Romana* – the peace imposed after Augustus' victories in Spain and Gaul.

Parts of it ended up in collections

all over Europe, and of course inside the Vatican, and it was not until the beginning of this century that the altar site was systematically excavated. Another thirty years passed before the whole altar was reassembled here like a giant jig-saw puzzle.

Ara Pacis

The upper frieze shows the procession in which Augustus (damaged) and members of the Imperial family, priests and high ranking officers of State took part on the day of the consecration. The quality of the sculpture is remarkable – many of the figures are clearly portraits from life. The floral decoration of the lower frieze is also superb. The Romans were skilful observers of nature – look closely at the details of the snake robbing a lark's nest, and butterflies, lizards and songbirds.
Open 0900–1300 and 1500–1800. Closed Sun. pm and Mon. all day. Entry fee. Metropolitana Spagna.

2 Arco di Constantino   7G6
Via di S. Gregorio Built in AD 315 to commemorate the victory three years earlier of the first Christian Emperor Constantine at the Ponte Milvio (Milvian Bridge) which is still intact, although closed to traffic, in the northern suburbs. Most of the sculpture decorating the arch was looted from earlier triumphal arches honouring the Emperors Trajan, Hadrian and Marcus Aurelius. The inferior quality of the reliefs dating from the actual construction of the arch in the 4th century is a demonstration of the artistic decline which accompanied the ebbing of Rome's greatness. Note the strongly pagan character of the sacrifices offered by Constantine; it is only fair to remember however that his final conversion to Christianity took place on his deathbed

22 years *after* the erection of his triumphal arch.
Metropolitana Colosseo.

1 Area Sacra Argentina   4E5
Largo Argentina This was the central part of the area known in Imperial times as Campus Martius, the Field of Mars. It was a rendezvous for races, gymnastics and martial sports and the name is perpetuated in the nearby Piazza Campo Marzio. The public gardens were adorned by temples, public baths and theatres. Mussolini had ambitions to create a modern parade ground here but after demolishing the labyrinth of medieval streets and houses which used to occupy the Largo Argentina, the remains of four Republican temples came to light dating back to the 3rd and 4th centuries BC. They are the earliest ancient remains in central Rome. Sunk deep below the surface of the modern city, they provide a vivid reminder of the archaeological treasures that still remain buried within the walls.
If you look down into the ruins just opposite the Teatro Argentina you will see the marble remains of one of the huge public lavatories of Imperial times – which in those days also fulfilled the role of a meeting place for relaxation with one's friends.
For permission to visit the ruins apply to Soprintendenza Comunale ai Musei Monumenti e Scavi, Piazza Cafarelli 3 (next to Capitoline Museums). Bus 64.

Largo Argentina

2 Basilica di Massenzio   7F6
Via dei Fori Imperiali This massive brick and concrete building, originally designed as law courts and assembly rooms, was begun by the Emperor Maxentius in the early years of the 4th century AD and was completed by his successor Constantine, who placed in

the apse a colossal statue of himself. The three great coffered vaults which survive give an idea of the huge scale of the building, but little conception of the fine marble decorations which formerly embellished it. Renaissance architects took their inspiration for many vaulted buildings from this basilica. It was damaged in the earthquake which struck Rome in September 1979 and is now no longer used as before for open air concerts and film shows owing to the danger of falling masonry.

Metropolitana Colosseo.

1 Castel S. Angelo   3D4

Lungotevere Castello Successively Imperial mausoleum, fortress, prison and Papal palace, the Castel S. Angelo is one of the most impressive buildings of Rome. The circular mound which forms the base of the Castello is all that remains of the mausoleum erected by the Emperor Hadrian shortly before his death in AD 138. It was encrusted with marble and surmounted by another smaller cylinder topped by statues. It must have resembled a giant two-tiered wedding-cake. The Castello was in use as a mausoleum only until the death of Caracalla at the beginning of the 3rd century. Then began a long history as a fortress during the numerous sacks of the city in the Dark Ages. The Castello took its name from a vision of the

Castel S. Angelo

Archangel Michael described by Pope Gregory the Great, which led to the building of a chapel dedicated to *S. Angelo in Nubes* (Holy Archangel in the Clouds) on the mound. The Archangel was credited with the miraculous saving of the city from a plague. The bronze statue of St Michael dominating the battlements was put there only in 1753.

In the Middle Ages, the Popes built a fortified elevated passage connecting the Castello with the Vatican. Pope Clement VII used it to escape during the sack of Rome in 1527.

During the Renaissance the Castello became a Papal residence and was decorated by many famous artists. It also contained the Vatican's Secret Archive until 1870. There is a superb view of the city from the battlements and also a terrace bar where you can have a snack after a morning's sightseeing. The public gardens around the Castello are also worth a visit.

Open 0900–1300, Sun. and public holidays 0900–1200 closed Mon. For details of Papal Apartments and Museum of Arms and Armour see *Museums and Galleries*. Bus 64.

7 Catacombe

The ancient Romans had a powerful taboo on burying their dead, or even the ashes of their loved ones, inside the city walls. The first Christians retained the practice of Jews and Egyptians of interring their dead in hope of a future life. They excavated many miles of underground galleries – no one can be sure of their exact extent but a well-known 19th-century authority calculated that the catacombs stretched over 500 miles under the countryside around Rome. The catacombs are filled with shelf-like compartments in which the dead were normally laid without coffins. The best known of these early Christian cemeteries are the **Catacombe di S. Callisto**. Entrance from No 110 Via Appia Antica, 1.6km/1mi from the Porta S. Sebastiano. Bus 118. Entrance fee.

Open 0800–1200 and 1430–sunset. Closed Wed.

Four vertical layers of labyrinthine passages cut into the soft tufa rock contain the tombs of tens of thousands of 3rd and 4th-century Christians, including at least five Popes. Visitors can also see the crypt believed to have been the original burial place of St Cecilia, martyred in her home in Trastevere, and reburied in the 9th century in the church erected to her memory above the traditional site of her house. The simplicity and freshness of early Christian symbolic art is attractive.

The catacombs were pillaged by barbarian invaders from the 6-9th centuries, and also by relic hunters, including some later Popes who carted off whole loads of remains to sanctify the churches they founded on the sites of pagan temples. Bones from the catacombs were sold all over Europe to credulous Christians anxious to possess some original saintly relics.

The nearby **Catacombe di S. Sebastiano** are entered just to the right of the church of S. Sebastiano, Via Appia

Antica, 2.4km/1½mi from Porta S. Sebastiano. Bus 118. This was the only Christian cemetery to remain a place of pilgrimage right through the Middle Ages when the Roman countryside became malarial and also insecure because of marauding soldiers and bandits.

According to an ancient tradition, the bones of SS. Peter and Paul were buried here for 40 years during the 3rd century in order to protect these relics during a period of bitter persecution. Archaeological confirmation of this tradition was obtained during excavations carried out after World War I. Graffiti dating back to the 3rd century and referring to Peter and Paul were found here.

Many other catacombs exist around Rome including several Jewish catacombs – one of them in the park of the Villa Torlonia – Mussolini's former residence – on the Via Nomentana.

The **Catacombe di Priscilla** (430, Via Salaria) lie to the north-east of the city and contain interesting fresco paintings dating from the 2nd century including the earliest known representation of the Virgin and Child in Rome. Opening times as for other catacombs.

2 Circo Massimo 7F6

Via dei Cerchi There was nothing dearer to the hearts of the ancient Romans than a day at the races – and the Circus Maximus was one of the chief entertainments of the city for a thousand years, from the time of the kings right down to the 5th century AD when the last races were presided over by King Totila, an invading Goth. The circus was the prototype of all racetracks in the ancient world. In its heyday 300,000 spectators roared encouragement to competitors. Racehorses were ridden without stirrups, but the most popular events were the chariot races which were staged for periods as long as 15 days at a stretch. The number of laps covered was recorded by the moving of seven large wooden eggs on the central *spina* or dividing barrier. The Imperial box, where the emperor and his family acknowledged the adulation of the populace can still be seen jutting out from the Palatine Hill. The 1200yd/1100m long track was later used as an arena for hunting extravaganzas or mock battle scenes in which hundreds of wild animals and casts of thousands took part. A water barrier separated the spectators from the lions, tigers and elephants. The Egyptian granite obelisks which used to mark each end of the *spina* were removed by Renaissance Popes to beautify their own new *piazze*; one now stands in the centre of the **Piazza del Popolo** and the other in front of the Basilica of **S. Giovanni Laterano**. For safety reasons it is inadvisable to visit the Circus after nightfall although the gardens are always open. Metropolitana Circo Massimo.

Inside the Colosseum

2 Colosseo 7G6

Via dei Fori Imperiali Originally known as the Flavian Amphitheatre, after the Imperial dynasty under which it was built, the Colosseo is still one of the most imposing structures of the ancient world. It suffered centuries of pillage by the builders of Medieval and Renaissance Rome who found it a convenient and almost inexhaustible quarry for building materials. It was not until the reign of Pope Benedict XIV in the 18th century that the Colosseo first began to be protected against further destruction and damage. The Church decreed that it should become a place of pilgrimage in memory of the thousands of Christian martyrs who perished in the arena.

The Colosseo was completed in AD 80 by the Emperor Titus – the modern name originated in a colossal statue of the Emperor Nero which once dominated the amphitheatre. Besides providing entertainment of extreme cruelty for audiences in Imperial Rome – including fights to the death by gladiators – the Colosseo became a military fortress at one stage in its history and was used for bullfighting during the Middle Ages. One Pope used it as a gunpowder factory. The Games which celebrated the opening of the amphitheatre went on for 100 days and included mock naval battles as well as the slaughter of 5000 wild animals and hundreds of gladiators. There were seats for 87,000 spectators. You could win yourself a slave here in a sort of Imperial raffle in which the Emperor distributed lottery tickets to the crowds. A huge sailcloth awning protected spectators from the glare of the noonday sun.

The Doric, Ionic and Corinthian orders of classical architecture are seen in their authentic original simplicity in the first, second and third series of arches on the exterior of the building.

Inside, the underground pens where lions and other wild animals used in combat against humans were kept, have been laid bare by archaeologists. A small museum contains exhibits which will enable you to visualise better the extremely well ordered seating arrangements and the elaborate theatrical machinery which kept the Roman crowds amused.

Open: 0900–sunset. Closed Sun. pm and Mon. Metropolitana Colosseo Bus 85 from Piazza S. Silvestro.

5 Domus Aurea   7G6
Via Labicana No 136 (Colle Oppio) (Nero's Golden House) We shall never know for certain whether Nero caused the fire that devastated Rome in AD 64 or simply profited from it to seize 160ha (400 acres) of the gutted city to build himself the most luxurious residence ever seen in Rome. All we can say is

that the legend about Nero fiddling while Rome burned is apocryphal, and that no other European monarch has ever carved himself out a larger slice of his capital city for his private use.

Apart from the façade covered in solid gold, the Emperor's pleasure palace had such refinements as baths with hot and cold running water either sea or fresh or fed from sulphur springs, hidden perfume sprays piped into the reception rooms, and a mechanical device for showering flower petals upon his banquet guests.

The gloomy chambers of the ruins of Nero's palace are mostly underground today. Trajan built his public baths on top of the ruined Golden House when it too was destroyed by fire in AD 104. Thirteen centuries later some of the rooms in the palace were rediscovered and the painted decorations caused an artistic sensation – it was the first time in over a thousand years that anyone had cast their eyes on the style that later became known as 'Pompeian'. Raphael used the Vatican *Loggie* as his model in the Vatican *Loggie* without knowing he had been copying wall paintings from Nero's Palace. As you walk through the cavernous *cryptoporticus* and through the octagonal hall a powerful pocket lamp will be invaluable in identifying the now much faded paintings. The famous Greek sculpture of *Laocoön* now in the Vatican museums was discovered here in pieces in 1506. It most likely formed part of Nero's splendid art collection.

Open: 0900–1300 Closed Mon. Metropolitana Colosseo.

2 Foro Romano   7G6
Via dei Fori Imperiali The entrance is in the Via Sacra running from Piazza del Colosseo near Arco di Tito. This was the nerve centre of ancient Rome, the gathering place where emperors and generals paraded in triumph with their spoils of war and their prisoners in chains, where great orators such as Cicero harangued the courts, where Mark Antony made his famous speech after Caesar's murder, where patricians and senators rubbed shoulders with the populace, where the Vestal Virgins kept the sacred flame burning, that homely symbol of the continuity of the Roman state. The paving stones of the Via Sacra (Sacred Way) are still intact and archaeologists have laid bare the foundations of many important buildings of the Republic and Empire.

As you enter, on the right are the remains of the Basilica Aemilia dating from 179 BC. In Rome a basilica was a public building used for transacting business, as a court of law, and simply as a meeting place where the cool marble halls provided welcome relief from the heat of the summer sun. The basilical plan later became the architectural prototype for the first great Christian churches.

Nearby stands the Curia, or Senate House. The present building dates from the 3rd century AD, but legend has it that the original Curia was founded on this site by Tullius Hostilius, one of the Kings of early Rome. The Curia was used as a church for many centuries until its restoration in the 1930s, which accounts for its preservation. The triumphal arch of Septimius Severus which stands at the North end of the Forum was erected by the Emperor in AD 203. Another smaller arch stands at the opposite end of the Forum – built by the Emperor Titus to celebrate his capture of Jerusalem in AD 70. On the inside of this arch you can see Roman soldiers carrying off the loot from the Temple, which was jealously guarded here in a specially built Temple of Peace until it was again stolen and lost to posterity after a sack of Rome by the Goths 340 years later.

In the centre of the Forum stands part of a small white marble circular Temple which was one of the key shrines of the Roman religion. It was dedicated to the cult of the sacred fire which symbolised the perpetuity of the Roman State. The goddess Vesta's fire was kept burning by six priestesses

Forum, towards the Capitol

known as the Vestal Virgins who lived a cloistered, but privileged life next door to the Temple in the *Atrium Vestae* (Vestal's House). Around the courtyard stand the pedestals of statues of Head Vestals from the 3rd–4th centuries AD. The institution survived by several decades the introduction of Christianity as the official religion of the Empire.

Open 0900 – one hour before sunset. Sun. and public holidays 0900–1300; Closed Tues. Bus 64.

2 Fori Imperiali 7F5

Via dei Fori Imperiali Entrance to Trajan's Market and Forum No 94, Via IV Novembre. Entrance to Augustus' Forum from rear in Piazza del Grillo. For permission to visit Caesar's and Nerva's Fora apply to Soprintendenza Comunale ai Musei, Monumenti e Scavi, Piazza Cafarelli 3, (near Capitoline Museums).

Many Emperors vied with their predecessors in their desire to leave lasting evidence of their wealth and power. Augustus claimed he had found Rome made of brick and left it marble – not an empty boast in terms of public buildings. Caesar, Augustus, Vespasian, Nerva and Trajan all built vast precincts or Fora to the northwest of the original Foro Romano. The site of these Imperial Fora is bisected by the triumphal way constructed by Mussolini, the Via dei Fori Imperiali.

Foro di Augusto lies on the right hand side of the Via dei Fori Imperiali going from the Colosseo to the Piazza Venezia, and can be identified by a huge tufa wall which divided it from the crowded and noisy Suburra quarter of the ancient city. The massive Corinthian columns are all that remain of the Temple of Mars the Avenger built by Augustus to commemorate his victory over Caesar's murderers at the battle of Philippi in 42 BC.

Casa dei Cavalieri di Rodi The Palace of the Knights of St. John of Jerusalem was built into the ruins of the Forum in the 12th century and later remodelled by a Renaissance Cardinal. It can be visited with the same entrance ticket and provides an unforgettable balcony view over the whole area of the Fori Imperiali. On the ground floor one of Augustus' porticoes is now a chapel.

Foro di Cesare lies on the left hand side of the Via dei Fori Imperiali going up towards Piazza Venezia. Only about a quarter of the area has been excavated but you can see the remains of a temple of Venus, and nearby a bronze reproduction of the original marble statue of the Dictator of Rome to be seen in the Musei Capitolini. The dreaded Mamertine prison where the ancient Romans strangled, beheaded or starved their public enemies to death was sited here. St Peter spent part of his imprisonment here and the adjacent church **S. Pietro in carcere** (St Peter in prison) commemorates the event.

Foro di Nerva was erected just to the south-east of the Foro di Augusto. Little remains except two large Corinthian columns known as the *colonacce* and the base of the Temple of Minerva which remained intact until relatively recently. It was dismantled by Pope Paul V at the beginning of the 17th century to build his impressive monumental fountain the *Acqua Paola* on the Gianicolo.

Foro di Traiano is easily the most ambitious and impressive of the Imperial Fora. Trajan's career illustrates the cosmopolitan character of the ancient Roman establishment. He was the first Roman Emperor to come from outside Italy – his father had settled in Spain and his mother was Spanish. He became governor of Upper Germany and then Emperor by adoption as Nerva's heir. His wide ranging military campaigns in what is now the Balkans brought back immense wealth to Rome. The Emperor's campaigns are illustrated in vivid relief on the Colonna di Traiano (45m/147ft) built in AD 113. The column has been severely damaged by atmospheric pollution in recent years. The top of the column marks the height of the former ridge joining the Quirinal and Capitol Hills which had to be levelled by slaves to enable the Emperor's Forum to be constructed. Some of the shops in the market complex are wonderfully well preserved. Trajan's creation, together with its temples, libraries and basilicas was considered to be one of the finest achievements of the ancient world.

Trajan's Market

1 Mausoleo di Augusto   1E4

Piazza Augusto Imperatore Augustus' family tomb was clearly inspired by the burial mounds of the Etruscans such as those you can see at nearby Cerveteri (see Out of Rome). The Mausoleum had a chequered history as medieval fortress, vineyard, formal Renaissance garden, bullring and theatre and concert hall, before being restored to its original simplicity by Mussolini who had plans, which never came to fruition, for using it as his own tomb.

For permission to visit the excavations apply Soprintendenza Comunale ai Musei, Monumenti e Scavi, Piazza Cafarelli 3, (near Capitoline Museums). Metropolitana Spagna.

2 Palatino   7F6

Enter through Foro Romano in Via dei Fori Imperiali. The Palatino, one of the original seven hills was inhabited from prehistoric times. In the days of the republic it became the equivalent of what we would call a smart residential area; later it was taken over by the Emperors for their own residences. After Decline and Fall had set in, part of the Palatino became a pleasure garden of the Farnese family. Vineyards and vegetable plots flourished among the ruins. Now it is practically the only part of central Rome which gives you an idea of the rusticity of the city which lasted for many centuries until modern urban sprawl began to swallow up the past.

The general impression of the Palatino is more important than its archaeological detail which is difficult for the layman to decipher. The Palatino can conveniently form the subject of a separate visit from the Foro Romano but if you can only spare the time for one visit, do at least climb up to see the exceptional view over the Foro from the north-east corner of the hill. This is not far from the point where the legendary she-wolf was supposed to have suckled Romulus and Remus. In ancient times a shrine marked the spot. In modern times a rather seedy she-wolf used to be kept in a cage but somebody forgot to feed her and the cage has now been empty for many years.

Tiberius was the first emperor to build his palace on the Palatino. The ruins of Domitian's residence are the largest single group of archaeological remains. They include a private stadium and Domitian's dining-rooms. Septimius Severus built baths as well as a palace here. There is a fine view to be obtained from the ruins of the former Imperial box overlooking the Circus Maximus racetrack. Try to visualize the scene below the garlanded Emperor as he presided over a day of hectic chariot races. If you find this difficult, fill in the details for yourself with a book called *Daily Life in Ancient Rome* by Jerome Carcopino, a former director of the French Academy in Rome, who gives a rich and detailed picture of what life must have been like in the ancient city.

Before leaving the Palatino do not fail to visit the **Casa di Livia** (Livia's House) to see some fine examples of interior decoration of a Roman house. The contrast between the delicate fresco painting and the grandiose ruins around could not be more striking. If Augustus and his Empress did not actually live in this house, this was the sort of décor with which they were familiar.

1 Pantheon   4E5

Piazza della Rotonda The first sight of the Temple of All the Gods, the largest and most complete building of ancient Rome to have come down to us, is a breath-taking experience. The huge concrete dome with its central *oculus* open to the sky represented a major engineering feat when it was constructed about AD 125. The date has been established from brickmakers' marks on the bricks, as reliable a dating method as silversmiths' markings in modern times.

Although the Pantheon seems a gloomy place inside take your time to examine what remains of the original decoration – a white marble cornice with a porphyry frieze. This was one of the key buildings of the ancient world and its influence upon European architecture has been immense.

The bold inscription on the pediment attributing the Pantheon to the Consul Marcus Agrippa (27 BC) is misleading. Agrippa's Pantheon was destroyed by fire and rebuilt 150 years later by the

Pantheon

Emperor Hadrian who modestly left the original inscription. The pagan Pantheon became a Christian church in AD 608 when it was rededicated to all the martyrs of Christendom. Twenty eight cartloads of bones of early Christian martyrs were scooped up out of the catacombs and reburied under the fabric on the orders of Pope Boniface IV. Later Popes and Emperors stripped the Pantheon of its fine gilded bronze roof and most of its interior marble decoration. The great bronze doors are the originals.

For centuries the Piazza was Rome's fish market, then in the 19th century it became a bird market in the days before the Italians had shot most of their wildlife out of the sky.

The pagan gods having long been removed from the niches inside, the Pantheon was considered a suitable resting place for the first two kings of modern Italy – Vittorio Emanuele II and Umberto I. Several famous Renaissance artists including the 'divine' Raphael are also buried here.
Open 0800–1200 1600–1800

7 Piramide di Caio Sestio   7E7

Porta S. Paolo Rome's only extant pyramid is a poor imitation of its Egyptian model. It was constructed by a wealthy Roman politician as his tomb in about 12 BC. The inscription tells us that one of Caius Cestius' jobs was the supervision of solemn sacrificial banquets and that the pyramid took 330 days to build. Do not fail to visit the nearby **Cimitero Protestante** (Protestant Cemetery) where Keats and Shelley are buried. (See entry)
Metropolitana Piramide.

1 Teatro di Marcello   7E6

Via di Teatro di Marcello This 20,000 seat amphitheatre was begun by Julius Caesar and completed after his death by Augustus. It was dedicated in 13 BC to the Emperor's nephew and son-in-law Marcus Claudius Marcellus who died in his early twenties.

During the Middle Ages the ruins were transformed into a fortress. The Savelli family rebuilt it as a Renaissance palace which then passed into the possession of the Orsini family. It has now been split up into apartments.

The exterior of the theatre was cleared by Mussolini of the small shops and workshops which had grown up under the arches during the centuries. Nearby you can see the remains of the **Portico d'Ottavia** erected by Augustus and dedicated to his sister. This

colonnaded building contained temples and libraries and was adorned with many works of art including the Medici Venus, found under the rubbish of the fish market which grew up around here in the Middle Ages, now to be seen in the Uffizi Museum in Florence. Remains of some of the 300 columns of the Portico can be seen sticking out of the pavement in the Via di Portico d'Ottavia or incorporated into nearby buildings. This is the beginning of the ghetto area where the Jews of Rome were once forced to live. A 13th-century Pope was the first ruler to decree that Jews should wear a distinguishing mark – a yellow O. Jews were not allowed to practice a profession or own land right up until the unification of Italy in 1870.
Not open to public.

Theatre of Marcellus

3 Terme di Caracalla   7G7

Via delle Terme di Caracalla (Baths of Caracalla) One of Rome's great contributions to civilization was the invention of the public baths. These *terme* were built in the reign of the Emperor Caracalla between AD 212-17 and functioned for about 300 years until invading Goths cut the aqueducts supplying the water. Over 1500 bathers at a time could enjoy the ancient equivalent of the Turkish bath, the sauna and the hot tub. The baths were decorated with rich marbles – later looted by the Farnese family. Two enormous granite tubs from the baths today form fountain bases in front of the Palazzo Farnese.

There were spaces for exercise as well as bathing, and the complex was serviced by an army of slave bath attendants. There were libraries, art galleries and gardens for bathers to unwind in after passing through the *calidarium*, the *tepidarium* and plunging into the *frigidarium*, the cold water swimming pool.

In summer open air opera performances take place in the ruins. The stage is constructed over the ruins of the

former *calidarium*. The classic opera to see here is Verdi's *Aida* with cast of hundreds supported by horses, chariots and sometimes even elephants and camels.
Open 0900 – one hour before sunset. Sun. and public holidays 0900–1300. Closed Mon.
Metropolitana Circo Massimo

5 Terme di Diocleziano 4G4
Piazza della Repubblica (still generally known by its former name of Piazza dell 'Esedra).
(Baths of Diocletian) the biggest public baths in Rome were built between AD 298–306 and could hold 3000 bathers – about twice the capacity of the Terme di Caracalla. The ground plan was roughly the same – a walled outer perimeter enclosing gardens, exercise rooms and hot and cold pools. The *tepidarium* was converted by Michelangelo into the Church of **S. Maria degli Angeli** in 1566. The remains of the *calidarium* now form the external façade of the church. Most of the remains of the *terme* are now occupied by the **Museo Nazionale delle Terme** (National Museum) one of the most important collections in the world of ancient sculpture, painting and mosaics, and sarcophagi. The setting is very appropriate as it was the custom in the ancient world to decorate public baths with works of art.
Metropolitana Repubblica.

7 Sepolcro dei Scipioni 8H8
9, *Via di Porta S. Sebastiano* The Tomb of the Scipios, discovered in 1780, lies on the left hand side of the street leading to the Porta S. Sebastiano and the **Via Appia Antica.** The cobbled road and the walled gardens on either side give some idea of how Rome used to look before the growth of the modern city.
The Scipios were one of the most famous family clans of Republican Rome. They were a family of conquering Generals – Southern Italy, Corsica, Algeria, Spain and Asia Minor all fell to their victorious Roman armies. But the most famous Scipio of all, Publius Cornelius, Scipio Africanus, who defeated Hannibal in one of the most decisive battles of the ancient world at Zama in North Africa at the end of the Second Punic War refused burial in Rome and was interred on his farm near Naples.
Ask the guide to take you to see the *Columbario di Pomponio Hylas* close by. The niches of this perfectly preserved Columbario (from the Latin, meaning

dovecote) held the cremated remains of 1st-century slaves and freedmen who worked for the Emperors Augustus and Tiberius.
Open 1000–1700. Closed Mon. Entrance fee.

7 Walls of Ancient Rome
The first wall, the so-called Servian wall, was built around and over the seven hills about 12 years after the Gauls sacked and burned Rome for the first time in 390 BC. Fragmentary remains of it are visible to the left of the main façade of the Termini Railway Station, and on the Aventino in the Via Di S. Anselmo. Although Rome quickly outgrew the Servian defences, no new city wall was built for six centuries until in AD 270 the Emperor Aurelian built his massive brick and concrete wall which still girdles the city. It is almost 19km/12mi long, but only encloses about 10sq km/4sq mi of territory. Today the original walled city contains less than 10 per cent of the population which has now spread out into an area of over 1300sq km/500sq mi of urban sprawl. One of the most imposing stretches of Aurelian's wall can be seen by taking the Via di Porta S. Sebastiano and following the wall from the Porta S. Sebastiano to the Porta Latina.

Aurelian Walls

BASILICAS

6 Basilica di S. Pietro   3B4

Piazza S. Pietro The first basilica on
the traditional burial site of St Peter was
erected by Constantine, the first Christian Emperor, and consecrated in AD
326. It was divided into five naves,
encrusted with mosaics gleaming with
gold, filled with tombs of Popes and
Emperors (Holy Roman), decorated by
the most famous artists. After a
thousand years the building became un-
safe, and after various attempts to patch
it up, Pope Julius II decided to rebuild,
entrusting the work to the renowned
architect Bramante, who demolished
the northern part of the basilica complex, earning himself the title of 'Mas-
tro Ruinante' – Mister Ruin – in the
process. Bramante and his patron planned a magnificent new church in the
form of a Greek cross, but died before
work had progressed very far. Raphael,
Michelangelo, and Carlo Maderno,
among others, all had a hand in the
design and execution of the new basilica, finally built in the form of a Latin
cross, and it was consecrated in 1626.

The full effect of Michelangelo's
dome is masked by Maderno's façade
when you view the basilica from the
piazza. The best view of the dome and
the exterior of the basilica, almost en-
tirely the work of Michelangelo, is to be
had from the rear in the *Giardini
Vaticani* (Vatican gardens) (see entry for
admission details).

Bernini's elliptical colonnaded piazza
(1656), perhaps his greatest single
architectural creation, encloses the vast
space in front of the basilica, where up
to a quarter of a million people gather to
see and hear the Pope on important
days. The obelisk in the centre of the
piazza was brought from Egypt by the
Emperor Caligula in the 1st century AD,
and used to adorn Nero's Circus. It
took 44 cranes, 900 workmen and 140
horses to move the obelisk into its
present position in 1586. One of the
entrances to the Apostolic Palace on the
right hand side of the basilica is through
Bernini's *Scala Regia* (Royal Staircase)
(not open to the public but you can
peek through past the Swiss Guards), a
masterful achievement in which he uses
tricks of perspective to heighten the
effect of depth and distance.

The centre bronze doors of St Peter's
were made for the old basilica by Antonio Filarete in 1433–45. They show
scenes from the life of Pope Eugenio
IV, who had to deal with the threat to
Christendom from the Turks. The reliefs contain an unusual mixture of
pagan and religious themes including
scenes from Aesop's Fables and Ovid's
Metamorphoses among the foliage,
while St Peter and St Paul are surrounded by inscriptions in Arabic. The
doors are 'signed' by Filarete in a delightful small vignette to be seen at floor
level on the back of the doors inside the
basilica. Filarete, wearing a distinctive
Florentine cap, leads his assistants in a
sort of congratulatory dance as they
wave in the air the tools of their trade.

To the left of Filarete's masterpiece
are a set of bronze doors by the modern
Italian sculptor Giacomo Manzù commemorating the Second Vatican Council. To the right is the *Porta Santa* or
Holy Door which is kept bricked up
except during Jubilee Years once every
25 years. The next Holy Year is not due
until AD 2000.

Entering the basilica, you cannot
help feeling overwhelmed by the richness of the marble decorations and the
sheer size of the building. It is 186m/
203yds long (St Pauls in London is
158m/172yds for the sake of comparison). The dimensions of other well-
known cathedral churches are marked
in inlay on the floor of the central nave
to enable you to gauge the scale of St
Peter's.

The centrepiece of the basilica is
Bernini's soaring bronze *Baldacchino*
(canopy) which took ten years to complete. It was dedicated by the Barberini
Pope Urban VIII who saw to it that his
heraldic bees were prominently repro-
duced among the decoration of the
swirling columns. Bernini also designed
the *Cattedra di S. Pietro* in the apse
which encases an ancient wooden chair
traditionally believed to have been used
by the Apostle, but in fact only dating
back to the time of Charles the Bald in
the 9th century. This highly theatrical
set piece depicts the four Doctors of the
Latin and Greek Churches (St
Ambrose, St Augustine, St Athanasius
and St John Chrysostom) together with
an assortment of angels and cherubs
floating on fake clouds while the Holy
Spirit hovers in the centre.

One of the most famous statues in the
basilica is the bronze of St Peter on the
right hand side of the main nave near
the Papel Altar. The right foot is deeply
worn by the kisses of countless generations of pilgrims. It was most likely the
work of Arnolfo di Cambio in the 13th
century – and is one of the few relics of
the old St Peter's.

Do not overlook the chapel to the immediate right of the main entrance as you enter the basilica where Michelangelo's *Pietà* stands spotlit above the altar, protected now by a bullet proof glass screen since a deranged tourist armed with a steel hammer attacked it in 1972 and grazed the Virgin's nose and did other damage. Michelangelo was only 25 in 1499 when he sculpted what few could deny is one of the most outstanding works in the whole history of European art.

If you have the time (and the energy) it is worth climbing up the 537 steps to the lantern at the top of the cupola to see the view of Rome, and also the unusual view of the inside of the basilica from the balcony which runs around the rim of the interior of the drum.

Access to the *Sacre Grotte Vaticane* (crypt) is via a door to the left of the Papal Altar. The crypt is all that remains of the old St Peter's and contains the tombs of 20 Popes including all those that have died this century, and that of the only Englishman ever to be elected to the Papacy, Nicholas Breakspear (in 1154 under the name of Hadrian IV). The so-called *Grotte Nuove* follow the curvature of the apse of old St Peter's. In the *Capella di S. Pietro* is a white marble slab dating back to the time of Constantine enclosing the traditional burial place of the first Pope.

Excavations carried out under the crypt in 1940–9 revealed a pagan cemetery of the 2nd and 3rd centuries AD with painted decorations of many tombs intact. The Vatican archaeologists also confirmed the existence of the *aedicula* (pavilion) on the Vatican hill described by an eyewitness about the year AD 200 and believed then to contain St Peter's tomb. Pope Pius XII reported triumphantly in 1950 'the tomb of the Prince of the Apostles has been rediscovered'.

Permission to visit the necropolis must be sought previously in writing from Rev. Fabbrica di S. Pietro, Città del Vaticano, stating your name, address of your hotel and telephone contact in Rome.

Open daily winter 0700–1800, summer 0700–1900. Crypt closes 1300–1430.

Bus 64

5 Basilica di S. Giovanni in Laterano 7H6

Piazza S. Giovanni in Laterano St John Lateran, the cathedral church of Rome adjoins the Palazzo del Laterano which was the site of the official Papal residence for almost a thousand years until the captivity in Avignon in the 14th century. When the Popes returned to Rome, the Holy See was established at the Vatican.

Little remains of the original basilica, founded by Pope Melchiades at the beginning of the 4th century on the site of an Imperial army barracks. The cathedral has been ravaged by fire (twice), sacked by Vandals, seriously damaged by earthquake, and was modernized for the last time in the 17th century by Borromini, so do not be surprised that it does not show its true age. The main facade dates from the mid-18th century and is heavily derivative of S. Pietro.

On a pillar just inside the basilica is a fragment of a fresco by Giotto showing Pope Boniface VIII proclaiming the first Holy Year in 1300. Above the Papal Altar, at which only the Pope is allowed to officiate, is a fine Gothic canopy by Sienese artists dating from 1367. A wooden table preserved inside the altar is said to have been used by St Peter himself to celebrate the eucharist.

A door in the left hand aisle leads into the *Chiostro* (cloister), a masterpiece of 13th century Cosmatesque decoration, carried out, as an inscription records, by a father and son called Vassalletto. The colouring and the imagination displayed by these mosaic artists is unequalled anywhere else in Rome. Around the cloister walls are displayed reliefs and tombstones recovered from the medieval basilica.

Adjoining the basilica is the 4th century *Battistero* (Baptistery) erected by Constantine in part of the baths of a palace belonging to a noble Roman family. The present building dates from the reign of Pope Sixtus III (432–440) and baptism by total immersion was practiced. The four chapels surrounding the Battistero are worth seeing for their mosaics. One, the *Cappella del Battista* has a pair of bronze doors which originally came from the Baths of Caracalla and make a curious musical sound when opened. The *Cappella di S. Giovanni Evangelista* contains some ravishing 5th-century mosaics of birds and flowers.

Across the piazza is the *Scala Santa* (Holy Staircase), all that remains of the ancient Patriarchal Palace demolished by Pope Sixtus V in 1586 when he built the present *Palazzo Lateran* as a pontifical summer residence. The Scala Santa was the ceremonial stairway of the old palace and according to medieval tradition it had been removed from Pontius Pilate's residence in Jerusalem

Basilica of St Peter

Basilica of St Paul, outside the walls

Basilica of St John Lateran

Basilica of St Mary Major

by St Helen, the mother of Constantine. The stairs are still climbed by devout pilgrims on their knees. They lead up to the *Sancta Sanctorus* (Holy of Holies), the former private chapel of the Popes, also known as the *Cappella di S. Lorenzo*. The chapel (always locked but you can peer through the grille) contains many valuable relics including a silver encrusted portrait of Christ whose image is said to be *acheiropoieton* (not painted by human hands). It was brought here from Constantinople before AD 750 and for centuries was carried in solemn procession through the streets of Rome to ward off calamities.

The Egyptian red granite obelisk in the centre of the piazza is the oldest, and the tallest in Rome. It was first erected in Thebes in Egypt in the 15th century BC, transported to Rome in AD 357 and finally brought here from the *Circus Maximus* (see entry) in 1588 by Pope Sixtus V to mark one of the hubs of his road network. Nearby for centuries stood the equestrian statue of *Marcus Aurelius* (see entry) now in the *Campidoglio*. The statue was mistakenly believed to represent Constantine, the first Christian Emperor, and alone of all the great equestrian bronzes of antiquity survived intact for this reason. The basilica is open all day from 0700 to half an hour before sunset. The *Scala Santa*, the *Battistero* and the *Cloisters* all close between 1230 and 1530.

Bus 85 from Piazza Venezia or Colosseo
Metropolitana S. Giovanni

7 Basilica di S. Paolo fuori le Mura

Via di S. Paolo St Paul's-outside-the-Walls, is or rather was, the second largest basilica in Rome after S. Pietro. A disastrous fire in 1823 gutted the building which had remained basically unchanged for 1400 years. Although rebuilt according to the former ground plan, the modern S. Paolo remains a coldly neo-classical temple despite the care and expense lavished upon its thirty year reconstruction. It took place at the nadir of Rome's unparalleled architectural history.

The altar canopy by Arnolfo di Cambio (1285) and the elaborate paschal candlestick are the only notable objects to have survived the fire. But do not fail to visit the exquisite 12th-century cloister which escaped unscathed. The variety and finesse of the stone carving, and the well-kept garden is an oasis of tranquillity and beauty among the desert of faceless suburbs around the basilica.

Metropolitana S. Paolo

5 Basilica di S. Maria Maggiore   4H5

Piazza S. Maria Maggiore The fourth of the patriarchal basilicas was erected by Pope Sixtus III (432–440) in celebration of the Council of Ephesus which proclaimed the Virgin Mary, Mother of God. The classical 13th-century exterior gives no hint of the riches you will find inside – the glowing purity of the original mosaic decoration dating from the time of Sixtus. Above the architrave are 36 mosaic panels of Old Testament scenes (a pair of binoculars will be of help in identifying them). The triumphal arch at the end of the nave is decorated with scenes of the Annunciation and the childhood of Christ, with special emphasis on the Virgin, portrayed as a Byzantine princess. The original mosaics in the apse were replaced in the 12th century by Iacomo Turriti, who also worked on the mosaics in the apse of S. Giovanni Laterano.

In medieval times there existed at the side of the basilica an oratory dedicated to the *Presepio*, or Christ's Crib. It was built to resemble the grotto where Christ was born in Bethlehem and was filled with precious offerings of gold, silver and jewels – all looted during the sack of Rome in 1527. Arnolfo di Cambio's original figures of the three Kings, St Joseph and the ox and the ass survived but most of Arnolfo's work was destroyed during the building of the *Capella Sistina* (named after Pope Sixtus V, not the same Sixtus after whom the Sistine Chapel in the Vatican was named). The surviving statues, beautiful examples of medieval mysticism, are in a grotto below the chapel. The gate to the steps is closed. Ask in the sacristy for someone to open it for you. The afternoon is the best time.

Opposite in the left transept is the *Cappella Paolina* (Pauline Chapel), built to house the tombs of the Borghese Pope Paul V and the Aldobrandini Pope Clement VIII. The semi-precious stones used for the sculpture – jasper, amethyst, agate and lapis lazuli – would be worth a king's ransom today. One of the sculptors was Pietro Bernini, father of the famous Gian Lorenzo.

On August 5 each year a shower of white petals is released from the ceiling of the chapel in commemoration of the legendary summer snowfall which is said to have inspired a 4th century Pope to build another (long vanished) church nearby on the Esquilino, dedicated to the Virgin.

Metropolitana Cavour or Termini

CHURCHES

The basilicas, churches and chapels of Rome are unique in the world both in number – over four hundred – and in variety of style. As they are still primarily places of worship rather than art galleries and museums, be discreet in moving around while a Mass is going on. Ladies should not enter churches in beachwear, however sweltering the weather outside. The four major basilicas are open all day from early morning but most churches close at midday to enable the *guardiano* to have his lunch and siesta (*pisolino* or *pennichella* in Roman dialect) and reopen about 1600. Opening times are only given if they vary from the norm. If you are looking at paintings, the best light is nearly always in the mornings.

1 S. Agnese in Agone   3D5

Piazza Navona. A dramatic 17th-century baroque façade by Francesco Borromini enlivens the centre of the famous piazza. The church's name refers back almost two thousand years – it is *in Agone* because it was built on the site of the Emperor Domitian's athletics stadium called the Circus Agonalis. Agone later became corrupted to N'Agona and then Navone. The story of Saint Agnes, who was martyred at the tender age of thirteen, is that she was stripped naked in a Roman brothel near the circus. A miraculous growth of her hair suddenly covered her nakedness and the scene is illustrated in a marble relief in the crypt. There are Roman mosaics under the church with some remains of Domitian's stadium.

7 S. Agnese fuori le mura   2K2

(Saint Agnes outside the walls) *Via di S. Agnese,* a turning off the Via Nomentana, 1.6km/1mi from Porta Pia. This early Christian basilica marks the catacombs and burial site of the teenage virgin Saint Agnes, stripped naked and murdered near the Piazza Navona. (**S. Agnese in Agone** (see entry) com-

S. Agnese in Agone

memorates the traditional site of her martyrdom in the centre of the city in AD 340.) This has been a popular place of pilgrimage for sixteen centuries. Do not miss the superb 7th-century mosaic in the Byzantine style, bursting with gold, which portrays the saint and the popes who built and restored the church.

On January 21 each year, Saint Agnes' feast day, two white lambs are blessed in the church and then handed over to the Pope as a gift. A community of nuns in Trastevere spins and weaves the wool into a vestment for bishops called the Pallium.

Bus 60 from Largo Argentina or Piazza Venezia (about 30 mins).

5 S. Andrea della Valle   4E5

Corso Vittorio Emanuele. A richly decorated baroque church with one of the highest domes in Rome after St Peter's. The architect was Carlo Maderno. In the nave are two finely sculpted tombs of the Piccolomini Popes from Siena, Pius II and Pius III, brought here from St Peter's in 1614. Under the dome, some excellent frescoes of the life of St Andrew by Domenichino. The church is perhaps best known as the setting of the first Act of Verdi's opera Tosca.

Bus 64

5 S. Andrea al Quirinale   4F5

Via del Quirinale. A gem of baroque architecture completed by the great Gian Lorenzo Bernini in 1671. Note the unusual oval plan. The rich marble, gilt and stucco decoration is theatrical, but stunning. Tricks of natural lighting emphasize the soaring figure of St Andrew above the main altar.

Metropolitana Barberini

5 S. Balbina   7F7

Via G. Bacelli (near Terme di Caracalla). Entrance from the adjacent former convent, now an old people's home. Between the United Nations FAO building and the Terme di Caracalla stand this quintessentially Roman church in a setting of ruins and cypress trees. Built originally over the ruins of a Roman house, it was extended in Medieval and Renaissance times. The superb Cosmatesque tomb of Cardinal Surdi, formerly in St Peter's, is the work of Giovanni da Cosma himself, and dates from 1291.

Metropolitana Circo Massimo

4 S. Bartolomeo   7E6

Piazza S. Bartolomeo, Isola Tiberina. The church was built in the Middle Ages by the Holy Roman Emperor Otto III over the ruins of the Temple of Aesculapius, the Greek god of healing. It was badly damaged in a disastrous flood of the Tiber in 1557 and restored in the baroque style. The well head in front of the main altar was certainly part of Otto's church, and perhaps marks the site of Aesculapius' original healing spring. If you walk down to the riverside to the left of the church, you can see the remains of the temple – blocks of marble in the form of a prow of a ship. Aesculapius himself is depicted on a bas-relief with a bull's head, staff and serpent. There are some amusing frescoes in a side chapel showing the floating mills which used to be moored in the river by the side of the church.

S. Bartolomeo in Tiberina

5 S. Carlo alle quattro Fontane   4G4

Corner Via del Quirinale, Via della Quattro Fontane. Also known as S. Carlino, this is one of the most original achievements of the great Baroque architect Borromini. The whole of the tiny oval church had to be designed to fit into the same space as one of the pilasters supporting the dome of St Peter's Basilica. It is a symphony of light, and undulating architectural rhythms. The counterpoint of dome and ground plan has inspired architects from many countries for over 300 years.

Metropolitana Barberini

5 S. Clemente   7G6

Piazza di S. Clemente, Via S. Giovanni in Laterano. Christians worshipped on the site of this ancient basilica, named after the fourth Pope in line with Saint Peter, right from the 1st century AD. For the past 300 years it has been in the hands of Irish Dominicans who are delighted to inform English speaking visitors about the complex history of their church on three levels.

The lowest level, 18m/60ft below the surface of the topmost 11th-century basilica, was originally the house of an early Christian called Clement, although not the Pope Clement to whom the church was later dedicated. Archaeologists have also discovered the remains of a Mithraeum, a gathering place for a popular pagan cult which flourished about the time of Christ.

The lower church, sandwiched between the Roman house and the present basilica, was rediscovered only in 1860. It is decorated with frescoes of extraordinary freshness executed during the 700 years that it was in use until its destruction by the Normans who sacked Rome in 1084. One of the frescoes, the 11th-century equivalent of a modern strip-cartoon, illustrates the cautionary tale of a jealous husband, and contains the earliest known inscription in the Italian language. The vernacular was obviously felt by the artist to be preferable to Latin for the somewhat earthy language of the story.

The upper church is one of the most perfect surviving examples of a medieval basilical church. Parts of the choir were rescued from the lower church. The rich gold, green and blue mosaic of the *Triumph of the Cross* is a stupendous example of the work of Roman mosaic artists of the 12th century. In a side chapel are fresco paintings of the life of St Catherine by a 15th-century artist called Masolino da Panicale.
Bus 85 from Piazza S. Silvestro to the Colosseo.
Metropolitana Colosseo.

S. Costanza   2K2
Via di S. Agnese, off Via Nomentana. This 4th-century baptistery and church with an unusual circular ground plan, is one of the earliest in Rome, and it is well worth making the tedious journey into the suburbs, 1.6km/1mi from Porta Pia, to see its stupendous mosaic decorations, which mark the artistic meeting point between the pagan and the Christian worlds. The visit can conveniently be combined with that of the nearby church of **S. Agnese fuori le mura** (see entry). The building was originally erected as a mausoleum for the Emperor Constantine's granddaughter Constantina (Costanza in Italian). Her finely sculpted porphyry sarcophagus was removed to the Vatican museums at the beginning of the last century.

The mosaics around the ceiling vault – vines, birds, flowers and geometrical designs – have no specific Christian symbolism, but they are one of Rome's rarest and most beautiful art treasures. The more conventional mosaics in the niches are of much later date but they too have superb floral borders.
Bus 60 from Largo Argentina or Piazza Venezia.

2 SS. Cosma e Damiano   7F5
Via dei Fori Imperiali This was the former library of the Emperor Vespasian's Forum of Peace. A 6th-century Pope founded the church and decorated it with some of the most striking mosaics in the city. The vivid colours of the robes of the two martyrs stand out against a glittering background of gold. The figure of Pope Felice presenting the model of his church was restored by a Barberini Pope over a thousand years later – and he included some of the bees which figure on his own family coat of arms among the flora and fauna.
Metropolitana Colosseo

Mosaics in SS. Cosma e Damiano

1 Gesù   4E5
Piazza del Gesù The chief Jesuit church in Rome was the prototype of the baroque churches of the counter-reformation – a rich and magnificent setting filled with polychrome marbles, sculpture, bronzes, gilt and *trompe l'oeil* painting calculated to inspire religious fervour. St Ignatius of Loyola, the founder of the powerful Jesuit order, is buried in the chapel to the left of the high altar. His tomb is covered with semi-precious stones and topped by the biggest known piece of lapis lazuli. The original solid silver statue of the saint was melted down to pay war reparations to Napoleon.
Bus 64

3 S. Giorgio in Velabro   7F6

Via del Velabro, off Via S. Teodoro
This mainly romanesque church takes
its name from the Velabrum, the river
swamp where, according to legend,
Romulus and Remus were found and
suckled by the she-wolf. It was built in
the 7th century on top of an earlier
church. The baroque interior was
stripped away in 1926 leaving bare the
original walls and antique granite and
marble columns taken from ancient Roman buildings. The stone altar dates
from the 13th century.

Next door to the church is the *Arco
degli Argentari* a small but ornate classical arch built in the reign of Septimius
Severus in AD 204 and named after the
moneychangers who gathered here.

S. Giorgio and Arch of the Moneychangers

5 SS. Giovanni e Paolo   7G6

Piazza di SS. Giovanni e Paolo
According to ancient tradition, John
and Paul were military officers in the
service of the first Christian Emperor
Constantine, who were recalled to arms
by his pagan successor Julian the Apos-
tate. When they refused to obey, they
were murdered here in their own house
in AD 362. Excavations under the basilica have revealed the remains of a
two-storeyed Roman house, used at one
time as a burial place – highly unusual
within the city limits. You can visit the
labyrinth of decorated rooms (entrance
at end of right hand nave) and see some
excellently preserved frescoes dating
from the 2nd and 3rd centuries AD.

The interior of the basilica is dis-
appointing late baroque. But the recently restored exterior, together with
the graceful campanile and the group of
monastic buildings around, creates one
of the most characteristic medieval
piazzas in Rome.

1 S. Ignazio   4E5

Piazza S. Ignazio The church of S
Ignatius, whose façade closely echoes
that of the **Gesù**, the chief Jesui
church in Rome, was designed by a
Jesuit mathematician, Fr Orazio Grass
in 1626 and decorated by anothe
priest, Fr Andrea Pozzo after 1685. Hi
extraordinarily skilful *trompe l'oeil* ceil
ing in the nave represents the entry o
St Ignatius into Paradise. The cupol
was never constructed but was painte
in by the virtuoso Fr Pozzo. Standing i
the centre of the nave and looking u
you would never know the difference.

7 S. Lorenzo fuori le mura   5K4

Piazzale S. Lorenzo, Campo Veran
cemetery. (St Lawrence outside th
Walls.) St Lawrence (who was martyre
by being roasted alive on a gridiron
was buried like many other early Christ
ian martyrs in a catacomb outside th
city walls. Rome's huge modern cemet
ery has grown up around the churc
since 1830. An allied bombing raid o
the nearby railway marshalling yard i
1943 caused heavy damage to th
church but it was restored after the war

The basilica is composed of two sep
arate churches which were built more o
less back to back and joined togethe
during the Middle Ages, when the fin
portico was added. The first church wa
constructed under the reign of Constan
tine, about 70 years after the martyr'
death, and rebuilt by Pope Pelagiu
between 578–90. This forms the chan
cel of the present church. It is deco
rated with a 6th-century mosaic show
ing the Pope offering a model of hi
church to Christ.

The second church was originall
dedicated to the Virgin Mary and date
from the 5th century – this now form
the nave. St Lawrence lies in the cryp
under the main altar – a superb exampl
of the art of 12th-century Roma
marble workers. Do not miss the near
by cloister of Pope Clement III, th
only double-tiered one in Rome.
Bus 492 from Largo del Tritone t
Campo Verano

1 S. Ivo alla Sapienza   4E5

*Palazzo della Sapienza, 40, Corso d
Rinascimento* Enter the. Palazz
through the Archivo di Stato (Nationa
Archives), formerly Rome University.

Borromini's imaginative church wa
completed in 1660 and is one of hi
greatest creations. Its hexagonal groun
plan is as unusual as the gilded spira
which tops the dome. Borromir
learned his craft the hard way – he wa

an apprentice stonemason and helped to build St Peter's as a boy of 15. His breakthrough as one of the leading architects of Roman Baroque came with a commission to design the church of *S. Carlo alle quattro Fontane* (see entry) on an awkward corner site. Even his arch-rival Bernini recognised Borromini's genius, and recommended him to the Pope to design this church. The virtuosity which Borromini displayed in creating an interior of such dramatic intensity in which there is hardly a straight line in sight was rarely equalled even by the great Bernini.

Open Sunday mornings 0900–1200. At other times ask the porter at the National Archives for the key.

1 S. Luigi dei Francesi   4E5

Piazza S. Luigi dei Francesi, Via della Scrofa The national church of France in Rome was built during the 16th century to the design of Giacomo della Porta. The façade is one of the few exteriors in Rome to have undergone a radical cleaning. The light colour of the travertine stone now contrasts strongly with the grime of most Roman church façades.

The treasure of this church consists of three works by Michelangelo Cara-vaggio, regarded today as one of the key figures in European painting. They dec-orate the chapel of St. Matthew, the fifth on the left hand side of the nave. Note his strong sense of light and shade and the hyper-realism of his style – he was criticized by his patrons for paint-ing Saints with dirty feet. His outland-ish behaviour led him into frequent trouble with the authorities and Cara-vaggio eventually had to flee the city after killing a man in a duel in 1606.

5 S. Maria degli Angeli   4G4

Piazza della Repubblica It may seem a strange idea to enter a Roman church in order to see the décor of an ancient Roman public bath, but the transverse nave is part of the original *frigidarium* of the *Terme di Diocleziano* (see entry). The *frigidarium* was transformed into a church by Michelangelo on the orders of Pope Pius IV in 1561. Eight giant red granite columns still support the origin-al vaulted ceiling. Unfortunately less than 200 years later the Neapolitan architect Luigi Vanvitelli changed the whole design of the church in accord-ance with prevailing baroque tastes, opening up a new entrance and con-structing a new apse. He demolished part of the ancient baths during his reconstruction work.

3 S. Maria del Priorato   7E7

Piazza dei Cavalieri di Malta, Via di S. Sabina Permission to visit the church is obtainable from the Sovereign Mili-tary Order of the Knights of Malta, 68, Via Condotti, near Piazza di Spagna. The church stands in the private garden of the official residence of the Grand Master of the Knights of Malta. It was rebuilt in 1765 by the great Roman engraver Giovanni Battista Piranesi, best known for his romantic views of the ruins of ancient Rome. It is one of the best examples of neo-classical architecture in the city where it all began. Piranesi also designed the small piazza outside the garden. Keyhole peepers will be rewarded with a framed view of St Peter's dome if they peer through the garden gate.

Bus 94 from Pantheon or Piazza Venezia to Piazza Pietro d'Illiria.

Twin churches, Piazza del Popolo

1 S. Maria del Popolo   1E3

Piazzo del Popolo The church had its origins in a chapel built on this site in 1099 perhaps to exorcise the spirit of the Emperor Nero, whose family burial place lay hereabouts according to popu-lar tradition. It is a real architectural palimpsest. The church was extended and embellished by generations of medieval, renaissance and baroque Popes and Cardinals and the artists they employed.

It has the unusual distinction of being the last resting place of a Pope's mis-tress – Vanozza de' Cataneis, mother of Cesare Borgia, who is buried in the chapel to the right of the high altar. Vanozza, a lady of great beauty and, in her later life, of great piety, was officially married three times as well as bearing at least three, possibly four, children to the future Pope Alexander VI.

In a chapel behind the high altar are two splendid renaissance tombs – the masterpiece of Andrea Sansovino. The figures of Cardinal Girolamo Basso della Rovere and Cardinal Ascanio Sforza recline as if asleep with their heads resting on their arms – a fundamental change in attitude from the stiff hieratic pose of medieval tomb effigies. The vaulted ceiling is decorated by Pinturicchio.

Do not miss the superb Chigi chapel on the left hand side of the nave. It was designed by Raphael for his millionaire patron the Sienese banker Agostino Chigi. The idea of a complete mini-church within a church was Raphael's original invention and he also drew the cartoons for the mosaics in the cupola.

Finally there are two stunning paintings by Michelangelo Caravaggio in the chapel just to the left of the high altar, depicting the Conversion of St Paul, and the Crucifixion of St Peter.
Metropolitana Flaminio

1 S. Maria della Pace　　3D5

Vicolo della Pace　The church was built in 1482 in fulfilment of a vow by Pope Sixtus IV that he would dedicate a church to the Virgin if she interceded to put an end to a war being waged against the Florentines. The graceful façade was added in 1656 by Pietro da Cortona. Above the arch of the first chapel on the right you can see Raphael's famous fresco painting of the Sybils – strongly influenced by Michelangelo's treatment of the same subject in the Sistine chapel ceiling.

From a door in the sacristy, you can visit Bramante's cloister, built in 1504. This is one of the seminal architectural achievements of the High Renaissance and was Bramante's first building in Rome – a true rebirth of the genius of classical architecture.

1 S. Maria dell'Anima　　3D5

Via di S. Maria dell'Anima　Two steps away from **S. Maria della Pace** stands the national church of the Germans in Rome (formerly including the Dutch and the Flemish). You can sense Northern order and cleanliness immediately you enter, from the obvious care lavished upon the church's upkeep. The chief point of interest is the tomb of the last non-Italian Pope before John Paul II, Hadrian VI, who reigned for one year from 1522 and came from Utrecht in the Netherlands.

1 S. Maria d'Aracoeli　　4F5

Piazza Aracoeli, (Piazza Venezia)　One hundred and twenty two steps lead up to the summit of the Capitol Hill where in classical times rose a temple of Juno Moneta (the Roman Mint, which incidentally gave us our word, money).

The present church was built in the 14th century. The name commemorates a medieval legend that Augustus, Rome's Emperor at the time of Christ's birth, was instructed to build an altar here to the Son of God by a local oracle. The legend most likely arose out of the medieval conviction that ancient Rome figured in the divine plan for the launching of the new Christian religion, and fell because of its unrestrained idolatry.

The interior is adorned with columns from the temples and palaces which once clustered upon the Capitol. The magnificent gilded ceiling was built to commemorate the naval battle of Lepanto which took place off the coast of Greece in 1571 and was one of the decisive battles of European history, putting an end to Turkish expansion and control in the Mediterranean Sea.

Among the curiosities of the church are a porphyry urn reputed to contain the remains of St Helen, the mother of Constantine, and the *Santo Bambino* (Holy Child) a 15th-century wooden image held in great veneration by Romans for centuries and credited with miraculous healing powers for sick children. Letters arrive from all over the world addressed to the Santo Bambino and they are left on the altar for a time before being destroyed unopened.

The major artistic treasure of the church is the series of scenes from the life of St Bernard painted by Pinturicchio (1486) in the Bufalini chapel.

S. Maria d'Aracoeli

5 S. Maria della Concezione　　1F4

Via Vittorio Veneto　Also known as the church of the Capuccini (Capuchin Friars), this Barberini church provides one of the more macabre experiences in

Rome for visitors who like that sort of thing. Five underground chapels are neatly decorated with the skulls and bones of more than 4000 Friars plus a few sons of noble families who died in childhood. The earth in which they were interred before being reassembled as wall decorations was brought here from the Holy Land. Some of the monks' skeletons are on display complete with hooded cowl. Very ghoulish! In the last century the church became notorious because of a certain Friar Pacifico who was believed to have foreknowledge of the winning numbers in the National Lottery. He was sent out of Rome by the Pope, but he gave a final set of winning numbers to his large following of pious punters.
Metropolitana Barberini

S. Maria in Cosmedin

3 S. Maria in Cosmedin 7E6
Piazza Bocca della Verita Originally a community centre for Greek refugees in the 6th century – the name may refer to a Greek word meaning 'decoration' – the church was enlarged in the 12th and 13th centuries, when members of the famous Cosma family of marble workers created the fine pavement, the choir and the paschal candlestick and also the marble *baldacchino*, or canopy, over the main altar. In the portico stands the *Bocca della Verità* (Mouth of Truth), an ancient drain cover weighing over a ton, in the form of the head of a river god. During the Middle Ages this was credited with the power of unmasking liars – anyone who told a lie while inserting his hand into the *Bocca* would have it snapped off. For centuries the *Bocca* was believed to utter prophecies and it is still one of Rome's most popular tourist draws.

1 S. Maria sopra Minerva 4E5
Piazza della Minerva The church takes its name from the ruins of a temple of Minerva upon which it was built in 1280. It belongs to the Dominican order one of whose most illustrious members, St Catherine of Siena (1347–80) lies buried under the high altar. The Dominicans were in charge of the Roman Catholic Church's Inquisition, and the tomb and statue of the Grand Inquisitor Cardinal Carafa, later Pope Paul IV, is a reminder of the terror inspired at one time by the self-appointed guardians of orthodoxy. The trial of Galileo Galilei, condemned by the Inquisition for maintaining that the earth moves around the sun and not vice-versa, took place in the adjoining convent. The church is so rich in sculpture and painting that space precludes an adequate description; among the most notable are: Michelangelo's *Christ bearing the Cross*, to the left of the high altar; the frescoes by Fra Lippo Lippi (begun 1488) in the Carafa chapel; the Cosmatesque tomb of Bishop Durand de Mende (died 1296) to the left of the Carafa chapel; and the tomb of Fra Angelico (Giovanni da Fiesole). Outside the church stands one of Bernini's most imaginative creations, a richly caparisoned elephant bearing on its back an Egyptian obelisk of the 6th century BC. Pope Alexander VII wrote the inscription on the base, to the effect that the elephant shows how necessary it is to have a strong mind to support solid wisdom.

4 S. Maria in Trastevere 6D6
Piazza S. Maria in Trastevere This may well be the oldest church in Rome, having been a gathering place for Christian worship since the pontificate of St Calixtus at the beginning of the 3rd century. The portico was the last main structural addition in the 17th

century. The mosaic on the upper part of the façade is believed to be about 700 years old. The women flanking the Virgin have never been positively identified, but the mosaic may illustrate the parable of the wise and foolish virgins. Inside the apse are some more outstanding mosaics which date from the rebuilding of the church in the 12th century. The subject is the enthronement of the Virgin. Underneath are another series of mosaics of the life of the Virgin by Pietro Cavallini. One of the panels illustrates the legend according to which a miraculous spring of pure olive oil gushed from the ground here and flowed into the Tiber on the day of Christ's birth. One of the streets leading out of the Piazza is still called *Via della Fonte d'Olio* (Oil fountain street).

Bus 56 or 60 from Piazza Venezia to Piazza Sonnino. Then walk up the narrow Via della Lungaretta. Beware of pickpockets and bagsnatchers as you walk around in Trastevere.

S. Maria in Trastevere

5 S. Maria della Vittoria   4G4
Via XX Settembre   This baroque church at the corner of Largo S. Susanna took its name from a miraculous painting of the Virgin (subsequently destroyed by fire) found among the ruins of a Bohemian castle during 17th-century wars of religion in Central Europe. The *pièce de résistance* is a composition by Gian Lorenzo Bernini for the Cornaro family chapel in the left transept (1652). The subject is *St Teresa's mystical union with Christ.* This soul-stabbing style is the ultimate in the baroque. An angel launches an arrow towards the heart of the Saint who swoons in ecstasy. The Cornaro family watches the happening from the wings.

Stendhal commented: 'Antiquity has nothing to compare with this. The ancient arts never depicted desire entering the soul.'

The superb quality of the sculpture is undeniable, but the unrestrained emotion may be too strong for modern aesthetes. The theatricality of the concealed natural lighting (best time for a visit is the afternoon, not the morning) recalls that Bernini was a keen student of the dramatic arts and even produced his own plays.

Metropolitana Repubblica

4 S. Pietro in Montorio   6D6
Via Garibaldi   From the terrace in front of the church you can see one of the most characteristic panoramas of Rome. The city skyline remains miraculously uncluttered by high-rise buildings and the scene below is not so very different from engravings of the same view published in 19th-century guidebooks. The church was commissioned by King Ferdinand and Queen Isabella of Spain in 1482 and contains some important 16th- and 17th-century works of art – among them a fine *Flagellation* by Sebastiano del Piombo, and a chapel by Bernini and his pupils where, for the first time, he used concealed daylight for trick lighting effects. In the cloister to the left of the church is the exquisite circular *Tempietto* erected by Bramante in 1502 on the traditional site of St Peter's crucifixion. You can see a hole where the cross is said to have stood, inside the crypt. The perfect proportions of this domed temple are an admirable example of the work of one of the greatest architects of the Renaissance, based on an accurate study of ancient buildings in Rome.

Moses Michelangelo

S. Pietro in Montorio

5 S. Pietro in Vincoli 4G5

Piazza di S. Pietro in Vincoli The church of St Peter in Chains was built in the 5th century to house the chains said to have bound St Peter during his captivity in Palestine. Later another set of chains believed to have been worn by the Saint during his imprisonment in Rome were added, and legend has it that the chains from Jerusalem and the chains from Rome welded themselves together miraculously. You can see the relics in a bronze and crystal casket under the high altar. The chief attraction of the church is Michelangelo's stupendous statue of Moses executed for the tomb of Pope Julius II (1514). The fury and majesty of the Old Testament Prophet come across with shattering directness. But the tomb commission was never carried out as originally planned and the tomb here is only a pale reflection of Michelangelo's original splendid vision. Other statues de-signed for the tomb are in Florence and at the Louvre in Paris, but the Master's hand is recognisable in Leah and Rachel, on either side of Moses.

5 S. Pudenziana 4G5

Via Urbana Tradition says that St Paul lived for a time in the house of a Roman Senator called Pudens on this site, but the church was not built until 300 years after the Apostle's death. Pudens' daughters Pudenziana and Prassede were converted to Christianity by St Paul and met martyr's deaths.

The crowning glory of this church is a 5th-century mosaic in the apse (unfortunately truncated during a 16th-century restoration) which shows Christ and his Apostles together with the two Roman saintly women. These rare pre-Byzantine mosaics, together with an even earlier example in *S. Costanza* (see entry) have a spontaneity and freshness about them that disappeared during succeeding centuries.

5 S. Prassede   4H5

Via S. Prassede The legend of S. Prassede is that she gave shelter to persecuted Christians and piously collected the remains of those who were put to death, and buried them in a well which is still preserved inside the church. She was the sister of **S. Pudenziana** (see entry) whose church stands nearby on the other side of the Via Cavour. The church, near the basilica of S. Maria Maggiore, was built in 822 and the chapel of **S. Zenone** provides one of the best examples in Rome of early Byzantine mosaic decoration. It was known in the Middle Ages as the 'Garden of Paradise'. Note the difference between the saintly living and the saintly dead in the artistic convention of the time. The living have square, not circular haloes.
Metropolitana Cavour

7 Domine, Quo Vadis?

Via Appia Antica 800m/½m from Porta S. Sebastiano the chapel dates from the 9th century but was rebuilt in the 17th. It commemorates the legend according to which St Peter, fleeing from Rome to escape death at the hands of Nero's soldiers had a vision of Christ. Peter asked the apparition: *'Domine, quo vadis?'* (Where are you going, Lord?) to which Christ replied, *'Venio iterum crucifigi.'* (I am returning to be crucified a second time) and Peter turned back to meet his martyrdom. The story was used for the title of the immensely successful novel of ancient Rome by the Polish 19th-century writer Henryk Sienkiewicz.
Bus 118 from Piazza del Colosseo

3 S. Saba   7F7

Via di S. Saba The original church was dedicated in the 7th century to one of the founders of Eastern monasticism. It was used by religious who fled the Arab invasions of Palestine. The present building was erected 300 years later. The Cosmatesque decorations include the main door by Giacomo Cosma (1205) and a fine mosaic pavement. In the aisle on the extreme left are a series of 13th-century strip-cartoons (to use the modern equivalent) illustrating scenes from the life of St Nicholas of Bari (who gained immortality in Northern climes under the name of Santa Claus). Three naked and penniless virgins are shown lying in bed. The provident Santa throws them a bag of gold to enable them to find husbands and to avoid a life of vice.
Metropolitana Circo Massimo

3 S. Sabina   7E6

Piazza Pietro d'Illiria This noble church was founded by Peter of Illyria in AD 422 on the site of the house of a Roman lady called Sabina (no relation to the later Saint of the same name from Umbria). The original doors carved from cypress wood are still in place – 18 panels representing scenes from the Old and New Testament. They are surely among the earliest surviving wooden sculpture in the history of European art. The basilica was well restored in the 1930s when the alabaster windows were replaced exactly as they existed in the 9th century. The interior has been stripped of most later accretions and, with its 24 matched Corinthian columns of white Parian marble gives a unique impression of the harmony achieved by the church builders of the first centuries of the Christian era.
Bus 94 from Piazza Venezia or Pantheon.

Trinità dei Monti

FOUNTAINS

4 Fontana dell' Acqua Paola 6D6

Via Garibaldi, Built for Pope Paul V by Giovanni Fontana in 1612 to celebrate the construction of a new aqueduct bringing pure water to the city, the fountain is a good example of Roman Papal plunder. It was built with marble and stone provided by demolishing an ancient Roman temple dedicated to Minerva in Nerva's Forum. The gushing torrents form the backdrop to a unique panorama of the city.

1 Fontana della Barcaccia 4F4

Piazza di Spagna The designer of this lovely fountain, now alas almost submerged in traffic on two sides, was Pietro Bernini, the father of the great Gian Lorenzo Bernini. The origin of the boat motif is probably the presence in ancient times of a 'naumachia' here – a building for the holding of mock naval battles, a favourite form of pageantry in ancient Rome.

Metropolitana Spagna

1 Fontana Delle Tartarughe 4E5

Piazza Mattei Hidden in a tiny piazza behind the Largo Argentina is this delightful composition by Giacomo della Porta (1584). The bronze youths are the work of Taddeo Lardini. Each holds a dolphin in one hand while supporting with the other a drinking tortoise. The four tortoises are now only reproductions. When one original bronze tortoise was stolen in 1979, the remaining three were also removed by the authorities and replaced by replicas.

Any bus to Largo Argentina

5 Fontana di Trevi 4F5

Piazza di Trevi The recycled water for the best known of Roman fountains passes along an aqueduct originally built by the Emperor Agrippa in 19 BC. A 15th-century Pope repaired the aqueduct called the *Acqua Vergine* (Virgin Spring) and 300 years later Nicola Salvi created this fantastic waterscape growing out of the side of a palace. Gods, goddesses, tritons and horses rise out of the sculpted rocks in cascades of water. One of the reliefs shows the legends of the Virgin Trivia (Trevi) pointing out the spring of the Acqua which rises about 20km (12mi) from Rome. Generations of tourists have thrown coins into the fountain perpetuating the tradition that will ensure their eventual return to the city. The coins that are not previously extracted by enterprising small boys go to the Rome city council and amounts to several million lire a year. The piazza around the fountain is crowded with tourists and souvenir vendors from early morning until late at night. The basin is a favourite stop for overheated tourists to plunge their aching feet into cold water.

Metropolitana Barberini

5 Fontana Del Tritone 4F4

Piazza Barberini Bernini sculpted his famous fountain of the Triton in 1643. Four dolphins support an enormous sea shell from which a reclining Triton or Sea God sends a jet of water spurting into the sky.

Metropolitana Barberini

1 Fontana dei Fiumi 3D5

(Fountain of the Rivers) see *Piazza Navona*.

Fountain of the Tortoises

Fountain of Trevi

PALAZZI · PARKS & GARDENS AND PIAZZE

1 Palazzo Borghese   4E4

Largo della Fontanella Borghese The first Borghese Pope, Paul V, bought this splendid Renaissance palace shortly after it was built for a fellow Cardinal in 1605. The palace is known as *Il cembalo*, for its curious shape resembles the harpsichord. It was here that Paul's nephew, Cardinal Scipio Borghese, founded his famous art collection now transferred to the Villa Borghese. Although the palace is not open to the public, the courtyard with its double loggias and hidden garden is worth more than a passing glance. The legendary Pauline Bonaparte, Napoleon's sister, who married Prince Camillo Borghese and enlivened early 19th-century Rome with her amorous exploits, lived here.

4 Palazzo Corsini   3D5

Via della Lungara (Trastevere) This 15th-century cardinal's palace, once the residence of Queen Christina of Sweden – who gave up her throne to embrace the Catholic faith – was rebuilt in the 18th century. After the French Revolution, Joseph Bonaparte lived here for a time. The killing of a French general in an uprising which took place near the palace in December 1797 led to the military occupation of the city by the French, the expulsion of the Pope and the proclamation of the Roman Republic. The upper floors now house the Galleria Nazionale d'Arte Antica, a collection of 17th- and 18th-century paintings and drawings, started by Cardinal Corsini in the 18th century and now the property of the state. For permission to view the collection apply to the Galleria Nazionale, Palazzo Barberini.

1 Palazzo Della Cancelleria   3D5

Piazza della Cancelleria Raffaele Riario, a Pope's nephew, won a fortune in one night from another Pope's nephew and had this most magnificent of Roman palaces built in the 15th century. A later Pope, Leo X, confiscated the palace from the Riario family who had plotted against him and installed the Papal Chancellery (cancelleria). The fine interior courtyard is believed to

have been designed by Bramante, but it is uncertain who designed the façade. All records to the building were lost in the sack of Rome in 1527. It is still Vatican property and concerts are occasionally held in the reception rooms.

1 Palazzo Farnese   3D5

Piazza Farnese The finest example of Renaissance architecture in Rome is the combined work of Antonio Sangallo the younger, Michelangelo and Giacomo della Porta. The palace passed from the Farnese family to the Bourbons of Naples and has housed the French Embassy since 1871. The courtyard, the famous Salon d'Hercule and the Caracci Gallery are open to the public briefly for one hour a week on Sunday mornings only from 1100-1200. Annibale Caracci and his brother Agostino decorated the sumptuous embassy dining room with scenes representing the Triumph of Love from classical mythology. The frescoes, executed between 1597 and 1604 mark the watershed between mannerism and baroque styles and are among the supreme artistic achievements of the city.

1 Palazzo Massimo Alle Colonne   3D5

Corso Vittorio Emanuele The masterpiece of Baldassare Peruzzi was built in 1532 for the Massimo family after their former house had been destroyed in the sack of Rome 5 years earlier. The unusual convex façade follows the ancient road called the Via Papale. It is enlivened by a deep portico whose columns recall the antique columns of the former palace. Architecturally it is one of the most interesting buildings in Rome for its dramatic use of projecting planes and curves. The palace housed the first printing press in Rome in the 15th century and also the Pontifical Post Office – an ancient privilege – reserved to the Massimo family.

For permission to visit, write to Prince Massimo, who claims ancestry back to the Fabii Maximi of ancient Rome.

5 Palazzo Quirinale   4F5

Piazza del Quirinale The Vatican used

to be regarded as unhealthily low lying and the Renaissance Popes built the Quirinal Palace as a summer residence on one of the seven original hills of the city.

For almost 300 years until the unification of Italy in 1870, it was a papal residence and it then became the official residence of the Kings of Italy; later, the residence of the President when the Republic was declared in 1946. The President's guard in their full dress crimson and blue uniform are a spectacle in themselves on state occasions. The gardens are immaculately kept and are the scene of a scintillating annual garden party given by the President to celebrate the National Day, each June. The well furnished rooms can be visited by applying previously in writing to the Ufficio Intendenza del Quirinale. The Sala degli Specchi (Hall of Mirrors) is particularly striking.

Metropolitana Barberini

Parks and Gardens

Until the end of the 19th century Rome was a city of walled gardens – formal and informal – which gave it a unique character.

Rome has now expanded practically everywhere up to the walls, but many elderly gentlemen can remember the days when not only did Rome end abruptly at the city gates and from St John Lateran they could look right over the Campagna, but the Aventine was still covered in vineyards and ancient convents. As in other European cities, suburbs have spread. Foreign diplomats and rich Romans pay fantastic rents for fantastic flats in Parioli; the new and fashionable suburb, which conveys no more feeling of being in Rome than in Madrid. But there are still exquisite gardens and parks, witnesses of an elegant past.

3 Cimitero Protestante 7E7
Via Caio Cestio The Protestant cemetery is sheltered by the Aurelian walls and is one of the most peaceful corners of Rome. This is the last resting place of the English poets, Keats (died 1821) and Shelley (died 1822) and such other famous non-catholics as an illegitimate son of the German writer Goethe and the Italian Communist Antonio Gramsci who died in a Fascist prison in 1937. After he drowned at sea and was cremated on a beach, Shelley's heart was brought to Rome by his friend Trelawney and buried here. Trelawney himself was buried 59 years later next to the poet. The cemetery's atmosphere is En-

glish because of its simplicity and well maintained trees and flowers. Travellers from many nations who died in Rome in the past two centuries are buried in this garden.

Metropolitana Piramide

7 Foro Italico
Lungotevere Maresciallo Cadorna The former pre-war sports centre of Rome in the northern suburbs was extended for the Olympic games of 1960 and contains the Olympic Stadium, an athletics track with seating for 20,000, and outside and indoor swimming pools. Open to the public mornings only

4 Orto Botanico 3D5
Via Corsini The Botanical Gardens in Trastevere were part of the gardens of the adjacent Palazzo Corsini, and are an oasis of tranquillity at the foot of the Gianicolo, filled with various species of trees, exotic plants and shrubs. The gardens and greenhouse belong to the University of Rome whose lack of funds accounts for the relatively poor state of upkeep.

Mon.-Sat. 0800-1345. Closed Sun. and public holidays. Admission free on production of passport.

7 Pincio 1E3
Piazzale Napoleone These public gardens were designed by the architect Valadier at the end of the Napoleonic wars on the site of the 'horta' or gardens of some well known noble Roman families of classical times. They are decorated with busts of famous Italians and the terrace which dominates the Piazza del Popolo affords one of the most famous panoramic views of Rome. The open air snackbar of the nearby Casino Valadier is a pleasant rendezvous for a moderately priced lunch or dinner with a splendid view.

Metropolitana Flaminio

Vatican Gardens 3B4
see Vatican City (pp.36, 62)

7 Villa Borghese 1F3
Rome's second largest public park (after Villa Pamphili) is 6km (3¾mi) in circumference, contains umbrella pines, a small lake and provides countless shaded walks. It is connected with the Pincio gardens by a bridge over the Viale del Muro Torto. The park was created in the 17th century by Cardinal Scipio Borghese and given to the city in 1902. At the northern end is Rome's Giardino Zoologico (Zoo), open daily

Temple of Aesculapius, Villa Borghese

0800-sunset (closed May 1st) which has a wide variety of animals, birds and reptiles on show. Although it does not come up to the standards of major zoos in Europe and America it provides an amusing excursion for children. (See p.24).

Metropolitana Flaminio

5 Villa Celimontana   7G7
Via di Navicella The west side of the Coelio hill is covered by a well-laid out public garden which used to belong to the Mattei family 400 years ago. There is a children's playground and the setting is a popular one for wedding groups who wish to be photographed for posterity. Metropolitana Colosseo

7 Villa Doria-Pamphilj   6B6
Via di Porta San Pancrazio Rome's largest public gardens (168 ha/415 acres) was acquired by the city authorities in 1971 and is open all day every day until sunset. The villa was built by a Pope's nephew in 1644 and now belongs to the State. There is a small lake and the remains of a water garden but unfortunately many of the statues which used to adorn the park have been vandalised and the state of upkeep leaves much to be desired.

However, the vastness of the park, its variety of shady walks, its splendid pine wood, makes this public garden one of the favourites of the area. Young children can cycle, roller-skate and feed the ducks. The elder children can play football and jog. Lovers can hide in the bushes. . . .

Any bus to Porta san Pancrazio or Gianicolo

7 Villa Madama
Via Macchia Madama This 16th-century villa originally designed by Raphael for the Medici Pope, Clement VII, is now the official Italian government reception centre for distinguished foreign guests. Heads of state are provided with a lavishly fitted-out guest apartment. The loggia was decorated by Giovanni di Udine and by Guilio Romano.

Permission to visit the villa must be requested from Ministero degli Affari Esteri (Italian Foreign Ministry) at the nearby Palazzo della Farnesina.

1 Villa Medici   1F4
Viale Trinita dei Monti Turn your back on the Piazzale Napoleone, take the road sloping down the hill and you are in Viale Trinita dei Monti. Just before reaching the villa you will see a column with an inscription commemorating the

Villa Medici

imprisonment of Galileo Galilei from 1630–3 by the Inquisition. This splendid Renaissance villa was grabbed by Napoleon in 1803 to house the French Academy in Rome. The garden is only open to the public for two hours a week on Wednesdays from 0900-1100. It is still worth making the effort to turn up on time to see one of the few well-kept Renaissance gardens in central Rome, complete with romantic 'bosco' and a love-temple. Metropolitana Spagna

4 Villa Sciarra   6C7
Via Calandrelli The garden and the villa partly bounded by the city walls was given by an American benefactor to the city of Rome in 1932. It contains a small children's playground and is well stocked with trees and plants. Its elegant loggia-belvedere is decorated with statues and fountains from an 18th-century villa in Milan.

Open daily until sunset. Any bus to Gianicolo or Villa Sciarra

7 Villa Torlonia   2J3
Via Nomentana The Torlonia family owed their fortune to supplying Napoleonic armies with victuals during their Italian compaigns. The garden of the huge neoclassical villa, which was chosen by Mussolini as his private residence in Rome, is now open to the public daily. Under the garden run a series of Jewish catacombs dating back to the second and third centuries AD. Bus 60 from Largo Chigi

PIAZZE

1 Piazza Di Campo Dei Fiori   3D5
One of the best fruit and vegetable markets in Rome is held here every weekday morning. The piazza used to be a place of execution. The statue in the centre is of Giordano Bruno, burned at the stake for heresy in 1600. *Beware the pickpockets and petty thieves.*

1 Piazza Navona   3D5
Probably the best known of Rome's piazzas, it owes its curious elliptical shape to the original *Circus Agonalis* or athletic stadium built by the Emperor Domitian. The name Navona is a corruption of the Latin *n'Agona*. Some of the ruins of the stadium can still be seen in cellars. Have a drink at the *enacoteca* (wine shop) on the Piazza and ask to visit their cellars. (Please, not in groups). There are also ruins in the tiny Via del Circo Agonale, halfway up the square on the right. During its long

Fountain of the Moor

Fountain of Neptune

history, the Piazza Navona has been the scene of feats of athletic powers, medieval jousting tournaments, water festivals (by flooding the formerly concave piazza) and pilgrimages to the scene of the martyrdom of **St Agnese**; whose church dominates the left hand side of the Piazza. It was also the scene of parades of elegant ladies and their gentlemen, a fruit and vegetable market and a Christmas fair that has now degenerated into a commercial festival. Hippies and drug addicts now frequently congregate in the square. The imposing **Fontana dei Fiumi** (Fountain of the Rivers) 1651 is the creation of Gian Lorenzo Bernini. The rivers represented are the Nile (whose face is covered, signifying the unknown source of the river when the fountain was built) the Ganges, the Danube and the Plate. The sculpted details of the lion, the palm tree, the horse and the various flora are worth observing. **The Fontana del Moro** (Fountain of the Moor) at the southern end of the piazza was sculpted by Giacomo della Porta in 1575, but the central figure of the Moor was added by Bernini the following century. **The Fontana del Nettuno** (Neptune Fountain) at the north end of the Piazza was completed only in 1878. The banning of traffic has added considerably to the enjoyment of the Piazza.

1 Piazza Di Pietra   4E5
The Piazza lies hidden just off the Via del Corso on one side of it is lined with imposing antique columns of a temple built in honour of the Emperor Hadrian. Now part of Rome's small Stock Exchange (Milan is Italy's main financial centre)

4 Piazza Santa Maria in Trastevere   6D6
See S. Maria in Trastevere p.105

1 Piazza Del Popolo   1E3
See S. Maria del Popolo p.103

1 Piazza Di Spagna   1F4
The Spanish connection is the Spanish Embassy established early in the 17th century. The famous Spanish Steps were actually financed by the bequest of a French diplomat to lead up to the French church of Trinita dei Monti at the top. For three hundred years this part of Rome has been the favourite haunt of foreigners. Anyone of note who came to Rome on the grand tour lodged here. The English poet Keats died in his rented room giving directly onto the steps, in February 1821. The prodigious display of azaleas on the Spanish Steps at the beginning of May each year is an unforgettable sight. Babington's English tea rooms at the foot of the steps is a venerable institution that has survived the years. You are served by Italian waitresses dressed as if they came out of Ye Olde Tea Shoppe and you can order tea cakes, muffins and waffles, if you should feel the need for solid sustenance during your sightseeing. On the right hand side of the square is the Vatican Palazzo di Propaganda Fide, where the work of Roman Catholic missions all over the world is co-ordinated and directed. It gave the word 'propaganda' to the English language.

Metropolitana Spagna

1 Piazza Venezia: 4F5
This is the result of some fairly philistine town planning to celebrate the unification of Italy at the end of the last century with the erection of the dazzling white marble and horrendously un-Roman Monumento Vittorio Emanuele. During the last war it was christened by the British soldiers, very rightly, 'the wedding-cake'.

VIAS

Via Appia Antica

The first of the great Roman consular roads was built in 312 BC by Appius Claudius and was the main trunk route to southern Italy and Greece, via the port of Brindisi. The Via Appia Antica is the only ancient exit from the city not to have been swamped by suburbs, although it has fallen victim to the murderous increase in motor traffic. Take the 118 bus from Piazza Venezia down the Via di Porta S. Sebastiano through the original imposing circular gate in the Aurelian walls, to the terminus at the Tomb of Cecilia Metella, which was turned into a fortress during the Middle Ages. It was the custom to construct family tombs along the roads leading out of the city and the remains of many funerary monuments are still dotted along the edge of Via Appia Antica. Some are now reproductions, after modern tomb robbers found the abundance of sarcophagi irresistible. If you fork left just before arriving at the church and catacombs of S. Sebastiano and take the Via Appia Pignatelli, after about 600m/yds, you will arrive at a sign marked S. Urbano. Skirting round the back of a modern villa you will see the small church of S. Urbano originally built as a temple in the sumptuous park of an ancient Roman villa belonging to Herodius Atticus, the millionnaire patron of the arts. It is a unique example of Roman garden architecture. Bus 118 from Piazza Venezia

Via Condotti

One of the smartest shopping streets in Rome stretches from the Piazza di Spagna to the Via del Corso. At 86 is the famous *Caffé Greco*, rendezvous of countless foreign artists, writers and musicians including Goethe, Mendelsohn, Berlioz, Baudelaire, Wagner and Liszt. The red plush interior retains much of its original charm. Metropolitana Spagna

Via Del Corso

Stretches just over a mile (1km. 5) straight through the city centre from the Piazza del Popolo to the Piazza Venezia. Flanked by palaces and churches of the late Renaissance and Baroque, the Corso takes its name from the horse races that were held there regularly for 400 years until they were banned at the end of the 19th century.

Via Della Conciliazione

The idea of cutting a wide approach road to St Peter's Basilica through the medieval quarter which grew up around the so-called Borgo di San Pietro, was debated for centuries and finally carried out from 1936 onwards during the years of Fascism. The Via della Conciliazione named after Mussolini's Lateran Pact with the Vatican of 1929, was completed for the Holy Year of 1950. Although it opens up a fine view of St Peter's façade, some of the original effect of arriving in Bernini's colonnaded square has been lost and the modern architecture seems very dull in contrast with the Renaissance and Baroque splendours which dominate the Via.

Via Veneto

The famous chic street with its international hotels and open air cafés, and the US Embassy, was built at the beginning of the century. In the 1950s it used to be a favourite gathering place for the jet set. Film stars, kings, and Roman princes rubbed shoulders as the photographers fought for the best shots. But the *Dolce Vita* charm has faded and the Via Veneto has become just another commercial tourist centre.

Via della Conciliazione

TIBER & ITS BRIDGES

1 Tiber and its bridges 4F5

The Tevere (Tiber) is a muddy uninviting river which in winter and spring rises and falls rapidly inside its steep embankments built at the end of the last century to put an end to centuries of regular floods within the city walls. Some efforts are being made to encourage boat trips for tourists during the summer. At the time of going to press there is no regular service, although an efficient water bus service would do much to ease traffic congestion along the Lungotevere on both sides of the river.

Ponte Cestio connecting the Isola Tiberina to the right-hand bank of the Tevere or Trastevere, was erected in the first century BC by Lucius Cestius. It has been much restored, the last time in 1892.

Ponte Fabricio (also known as the Ponte dei Quattro Capi or Bridge of the Four Heads) connects the city with the Isola Tiberina. It is the second oldest bridge in Rome built in 62 BC. The inscription commemorating the builder Lucius Fabricius has survived almost intact.

Ponte Milvio In the northern suburbs of the city this is the oldest existing bridge across the Tiber dating from 109 BC, but it was partly destroyed by Garibaldi in 1849 to halt the French troops advancing on Rome. It was then restored the following year. Since 1978 the bridge has been closed to motor traffic for safety reasons. On this bridge in AD 312, one of the decisive battles of the ancient world was fought between the Emperors Constantine and Maxentius. Constantine won and became the first Christian Emperor of Rome.

Ponte Sant Angelo is opposite the Castel S. Angelo and the three central arches are the ancient remains of the Ponte Elia which originally led to Hadrian's family mausoleum. Pope Clement VII commissioned the statues of SS Peter and Paul in 1535 while the ten statues of angels, one of the finest creations of Roman baroque were designed by Bernini and executed by his pupils in 1668.

Ponte Sisto was built by Pope Sixtus IV in 1474 on the site of a bridge originally built by Marcus Aurelius which collapsed during the Middle Ages. The aim was to relieve the growing pressure on pilgrim traffic across the Tiber to the Vatican during Holy Years.

Ponte S. Angelo

Ponte Fabricio

Ponte Cestio

OUTSIDE ROME

Sea Bathing The sea near Rome has reached a high level of pollution and you should *not* bathe at **Ostia** or **Fiumicino** the nearest sea resorts. There are good sandy beaches at **Fregene** to the north of the city and towards Anzio to the south. All beaches near Rome tend to be very overcrowded at weekends during summer. The best excursion for a weekend by the sea is the small resort of **Sperlonga** (127km/79mi by road) just south of Terracina about halfway between Rome and Naples.

Colli Albani The area to the immediate south-east of the city is known as the **Castelli Romani**, a series of fortified towns and villages most of which can trace back their foundation to before Christ. The **Colli Albani** (Alban Hills) are extinct volcanoes and two former craters form the Lakes of Nemi and Albano. The highest point is Monte Cavo (949m/3100ft). The Castelli have been overbuilt in recent years, but they still make a pleasant excursion in summer if you wish to escape the heat of the city. The more interesting towns are listed below.

Castel Gandolfo

Lazio (25km/15.5mi) Situated on the rim of the crater, and overlooking Lake Albano, the village is known mainly on account of its choice as a Papal Summer residence. The Palazzo Papale was built by Pope Urban VIII in 1624 and it has been used by most pontiffs since then. The Papal Villa has a magnificent park (not open to the public) and contains the telescopes of the Vatican Observatory. Castel Gandolfo was built according to legend over the ruins of Alba Longa, founded by Ascanius, son of Aeneas, and was the chief town of the Latin League in the days of the Kings of Rome.

Cerveteri

Lazio (46km/25.5mi) was known by the Etruscans as **Caere** and a visit to the necropolis is an essential complement to a visit to the Etruscan museum of the Villa Giulia in Rome. The tomb area is approached by a cypress-lined avenue about 2km/1mi from the village. The variety of the tombs in this city of the dead dating as far back as the 6th century BC is astonishing. The tombs faithfully reflect the houses of the Etruscans which were made of less durable materials and have long since disappeared; they are curiously intimate and welcoming places. Some contain the remains of paintings and reliefs – ask the guide to show you the **Tomba dell'Alcova** and the **Tomba dei Rilievi.** The famous Etruscan vase of *Euphronios*, now in the Metropolitan Museum of Art in New York was dug up here by tomb robbers in the 1960s. From ancient times, the tombs of the Etruscans have provided a rich source of loot for treasure hunters – a short walk into the countryside will reveal from the freshly dug ground that the illicit search for archaeological remains continues.

The Necropolis is open 1000–1600 in winter and 0900–1300 and 1600–1900 in summer, closed Mon. Allow 2 hours for visit.

If you feel hungry after communing with the spirits of the Etruscans try the Trattoria *Da Gerardo* in the village on the right hand side as you enter the main square. Gerardo is a poet as well as a provider of good food and you may be lucky enough to hear him recite his verse as you sip your *digestivo*. Gerardo grows all his own fruit and vegetables and his wine cellar is installed inside an Etruscan tomb.

Train to Cerveteri 50 mins from Termini on main Rome-Livorno line.

By road along the Roma-Civitavecchia autostrada A12, or by the Via Aurelia N1.

EUR (pronounced AY-OO-AHR) stands for *Esposizione Universale Romana* and was destined by Mussolini in 1938 as a permanent exhibition in honour of the glories of Rome. It was planned for completion in 1942 but World War II prevented this grandiose design – the 'Olympics of Civilization' as it was pompously called by the Fascists – from being carried out. After the war, the area was developed as a satellite city – with spacious parks and wide streets – the only conscious piece of urban planning around Rome, where illegal building developments now outnumber the legal ones.

Pier Luigi Nervi's **Palazzo dello Sport** was built for the 1960 Rome Olympic Games.

The **Museo della Civiltà Romana** (Museum of Roman civilization) is worth seeing if only for its large scale model of the buildings of Ancient Rome (see p.55) and for the series of plaster casts taken from Trajan's Column which enable the reliefs to be seen in much greater detail than *in situ*.

There is a boating lake surrounded by over a thousand flowering cherry

trees given by the city of Tokyo.
EUR is linked by the Metropolitana to Termini (journey time 10 mins). Stations: EUR Marconi and EUR Fermi.

Palazzo di Lavoro, EUR

Frascati

Lazio (22km/14mi) is famous for its light white wines which you can taste in any of the cellars scattered throughout the town. Visit the park of the **Villa Aldobrandini** (open daily except Sundays 0900–1300, you need a permit from the Azienda di Soggiorno, Piazza Marconi) to get an idea of the sort of country estate that rich and powerful Roman families have built themselves since time immemorial in the Castelli. There is an incomparable view over Rome from the terraces. The villa was built for Cardinal Aldobrandini, nephew of Pope Clement VII in 1598. Cicero had a villa up the hill at *Tusculum* and the ruins of the Roman town are worth a short visit.

Genzano

Lazio (30km/19mi) is the starting point for a visit to the Lake of Nemi, called 'Diana's mirror' in ancient times. In May the wooded slopes provide an abundant supply of 'fragolini' (wild strawberries) a favourite delicacy at Roman dining tables since the days of Nero. By the lakeside, a small museum contains the remains of two huge Roman ships 71×24m/250×79ft, built in AD 37 in the reign of the Emperor Caligula and used for elaborate water festivals on the lake. The vessels were dredged from the lake in 1940 but were unfortunately severely damaged by fire during World War II. They were fascinating examples of Roman naval architecture.

Lago di Bracciano

Lazio (39km/24mi) Lake Bracciano lies in the craters of a group of extinct volcanoes north west of Rome. A number of sailing clubs have grown up around its shores and fish from the lake is served at pleasant waterside trattorie in **Trevignano** and **Anguillara Sabazia**, two picturesque villages on the north and south shores. The town of **Bracciano** is worth a visit to see the Renaissance **Castello**, built by the Orsini family, open Thurs., Sat. and Sun. 1000–1200 and 1500–1700. The road around the lake is 31km/19mi and there are agreeable walks to be made on the hills around.

By road the fastest route is by the *Cassia bis superstrada* which is marked to Viterbo and which lies between the Via Flaminia and the Via Cassia. Access from the Anulare. At 35km/22mi turn left to Trevignano.

Marino

Lazio (28km/17mi) belonged to the princely Colonna family. It is the centre of an important white wine growing area and stages a rowdy wine festival on the first Sunday in October.

Buses to most parts of the Castelli leave regularly from Via Carlo Felice, opposite the Basilica of S. Giovanni in Laterano. (Metropolitana S. Giovanni) There is a rapid and frequent train service to Frascati from Termini.

Monte Cassino

Lazio (139km/86mi) The abbey was founded by St Benedict in 529 and he died here in 543. The head monastery of the Benedictine order became one of the most famous and richest religious foundations in Europe during the Middle Ages and the library contains a unique collection of ancient and medieval manuscripts. The abbey was almost totally destroyed (for the fourth time in its history) during World War II in the battle for the strategic route to Rome during the winter of 1943–4. It has since been faithfully reconstructed and attracts many tourists and pilgrims who also come to visit the large Polish, British, American and German war cemeteries.

Open 0730–1230 and 1530–sunset
Train from Termini to Cassino and thence by bus or taxi (9km/5.5mi).
By road Autostrada Roma-Napoli A2. Exit at Cassino and take the winding road up the mountain.

Ninfa

Lazio (70km/43.5mi) The medieval village of Ninfa was abandoned because of the malaria which raged for hundreds of years in much of the swampland (reclaimed during Fascism) to the southeast of Rome. But the owners of the village, the princely Caetani family, transformed the ruins into a romantic water-garden. It is open to the public only on the first Saturday and Sunday of each month from April to September, but is one of the great neglected sights around Rome. A clear fastrunning stream passes through the immaculately tended gardens which are filled with flowering shrubs and trees. The World Wildlife Fund provides guides.

Nearby, the medieval hillside village of **Norma** commands a stupendous view of the coastal plain. Ten minutes away are the ruins of **Norba**, a Volscian town whose imposing walls date from the 4th century BC The medieval Cistercian Abbey of Valvisciolo can be visited near Ninfa, as can the 14th-century Caetani Castello complete with drawbridge at Sermoneta.

By road Via Appia Nuova to Cisterna, turn left 3km/2mi after Cisterna.

Bus to Cisterna from Via Carlo Felice, opposite Basilica di S. Giovanni in Laterano.

Orvieto

Umbria (121km/75mi) Orvieto is an exceptionally sited hilltop town of Etruscan origin which lies within easy reach of Rome. An overnight stay at least is advisable.

The Gothic **Duomo** (cathedral) was begun in 1290 to celebrate the miracle of Bolsena, a medieval religious happening which took place in a village on the shores of Lake Bolsena, when a doubting priest saw the Host spouting blood as he was celebrating Mass.

Generations of architects, sculptors, stonemasons, artists and mosaic workers toiled during several hundred years to complete the Duomo, one of the finest buildings in central Italy; the frescoes painted by Luca Signorelli in the **Cappella della Madonna di S. Brizio** during the latter half of the 15th century are worth particular attention. The vivid strength of his figure painting in the Last Judgement scenes gives a foretaste of Michelangelo.

Just wandering around the streets of this Umbrian provincial town is a pleasure. There is a good choice of hotels and trattorie. If you feel well off, stay at **La Badia** a converted 12th-century

Duomo, Orvieto

abbey with a stupendous view over the town. (Tel: 0763·90359). Or on a more modest, but still comfortable, level try a former Papal villa now run as an excellent hotel and restaurant 6km/4mi along the road to Viterbo, the **Résidence Buon Viaggio,** (Tel: 0763 5502)

Train from Termini to Orvieto Scalo

By road take the Roma – Firenze Autostrada A 1 direct to Orvieto.

Ostia Antica

Lazio (28km/17mi) A visit to the ruins of the ancient seaport of Rome is one of the most interesting excursions around the city, as it gives a much better idea of Roman urban life than any of the random remains which have survived within the city walls. The sea has receded more than a mile since ancient times, and the River Tiber changed its course after a flood in 1575. But the general layout of the port city together with theatre, forum, temples, public baths, shops and private houses many with their original mosaic or inlaid marble floors, is clear from the moment you set foot in the **Decumanus Maximus,** or Main Street, whose original paving stones are still rutted by chariot wheels.

Past the theatre, look out for the **Via Diana** and the **Thermopolium** (the nearest Latin could get to a bar) with its marble drinks counter and paintings of food and beverages for sale. (Incidentally the modern bar is installed under one of the arches of the theatre, if you get thirsty).

The Romans coped with urban over-crowding by building multi-storey apartment houses. The blocks were called *insulae* or 'islands' and the remains of several such high-rise buildings stand near the *Thermopolium*.

A small museum (enquire for opening times) contains some interesting pieces of sculpture, mosaics, and sar-cophagi unearthed during the excavations which are still continuing. In sum-mer open air performances of classical plays are given in the ancient theatre.
Open 0900–one hour before sunset. Closed Mon. and most public holidays. You can drive your car into a park inside the excavations on payment of a small additional fee.
Train frequent service from Roma Lido Stazione (Metropolitana Piramide)
By road take the Via del Mare (near S. Paolo fuori le Mura), Italy's first motor-way (where Mussolini used to like speeding in a souped-up Lagonda) and turn off at Ostia Antica.

Palestrina

Lazio (38km/24mi) This medieval town perched on a mountain side east of Rome was an important place of pagan pilgrimage in antiquity called **Praeneste**. A temple dedicated to the goddess Fortune existed here from the 6th century BC, and there was a famous oracle. The vast sanctuary was recon-structed towards the end of the 2nd century BC on six levels terraced out of the mountainside. In the Middle Ages the Colonna family built a palace in the ruins and this now houses the *Museo Archeologico Prenestino* (open 0900–1400 daily except Mon. and public holi-days). It is worth a visit just to see the marvellous mosaic of the river Nile, dating perhaps from the 1st century BC, and there are numerous objects reco-vered by archaeologists from the sanc-tuary.
By train one hour journey – frequent services from Stazione Roma Laziali, Via Giolitti, at side of Stazione Termini. By road the Via Prenestina which fol-lows the route used by pilgrims to the Goddess Fortune in ancient times now trails through miles of dreary suburbs before emerging into the countryside.

Subiaco

Lazio (72km/45mi) A mountain village made famous by St Benedict who in the 6th century founded his religious order of the Benedictines here under the rule *ora et labora* ('pray and work'). He and

his twin sister Scolastica both founded convents and monasteries here. The monks will show you a cave where St Benedict lived for a time as a hermit.

The *Monastero di S. Benedetto* and the *Monastero di S. Scolastica* lie 3 km/2mi from the village on the road to Frosinone.

Tarquinia

Lazio (97km/60mi) For those bitten by the desire to know more about the Etruscans, Tarquinia is a rewarding place to visit. The two Kings of Rome called Tarquin came from here, and the city flourished between the 6th–1st cen-turies BC. The **Museo Nazionale** is installed in a fine Renaissance Palazzo, the **Palazzo Vitelleschi** and contains a good collection of vases and artefacts including the memorable **Cavalli alati** (Winged horses), part of the pediment of an Etruscan temple. Ask at the Museo for a guide to accompany you to the Necropolis, 4km/2.5mi away, to see the painted tombs. The richness, diver-sity and directness of the wall paintings dating from the 6th–3rd centuries BC inside these tombs are stunning. Damp and mildew and an escalating number of visitors have created a serious conser-vation problem, so hurry before time erases these incomparable pre-Roman works of art.
Open 0900–1500 daily except Mon. and public holidays.
By rail: from Stazione Termini (Livor-no line)
By road follow the signs to Fiumicino airport and just before the airport take the Autostrada Roma-Civitavecchia A16, then follow the Via Aurelia along the coast to Tarquinia.

Tivoli

Lazio (31km/19mi) The ancient Roman Tibur has always been a favourite hill resort for Romans, but it is now threatened by uncontrolled urban sprawl. Two summer palaces, one now in ruins, as it was built 1800 years ago by the Emperor Hadrian, and the other with a notable Renaissance garden are worth seeing.

The **Villa d'Este**, originally a con-vent, was constructed by Cardinal Ippo-lito d'Este in 1550. In front he created one of the great water-gardens of Europe with more than 500 fountains fed from an aqueduct that passes under the town. One fountain used to play organ music through the 16th century equivalent of a modern juke-box – a hydraulic organ. In summer the gar-dens are illuminated in the evening, but

beware the crowds. The Villa d'Este is now alas considered by tour operators to be one of the major sights of Rome and draws cohorts of tourist buses.
Open 0900–1830 and from May to September 2000–2230. Closed Mon.

The **Villa Adriana** (Hadrian's Villa) was the largest and richest of all Roman Imperial villas. It was built between AD 118–34 at the foot of the mountain on which Tivoli is situated. Hadrian wanted to recreate some of the places which had most impressed him on his travels in the Empire – so there were imitations of famous buildings in Athens, a landscaped garden representing the Vale of Tempe in Thessaly in Greece, and a canal and temple to Serapis he had seen in Egypt. Hadrian died shortly after the completion of his sumptuous villa, and over the centuries the Emperor's grandiose pleasure park was gradually despoiled of its statuary, marbles and mosaics. Cardinal Ippolito d'Este did not hesitate to use the Villa as a quarry for building his own residence up the hill.

Systematic excavations were carried out from the time of Pope Alexander VI at the end of the 15th century. Hundreds of works of art dug up here have found their way into museums and collections all over Europe.

Allow at least 2–3 hours to wander around one of the world's most impressive archaeological sites.
Open 0900 to one hour before sunset. Closed Mon.
The Villa lies about 6km/4mi before Tivoli off to the right of the main Rome-Tivoli road (N5). If you wish to avoid the journey through dreary suburbs take the Roma-L'Aquila Autostrada A24 and turn off after 26km/16mi at the TIVOLI sign.

Veio

Lazio (20km/12mi) The ancient Veii was an important Etruscan town, the scene of fierce battles in the days when Rome was fighting to gain its supremacy over the Etruscans. Some idea of its importance may be gauged from the fact that the city walls measured over 8km/5mi in circumference. The ruins of Veii lie in a dramatic site near a ravine. The famous *Apollo of Veii* now in the *Villa Giulia* Etruscan museum was found here near the ruins of a temple of Apollo.
Bus 201 from Ponte Milvio to Isola Farnese. Then take the road towards the waterfall.
By car take the Via Cassia for 17km/10.5mi and turn right to the village of Isola Farnese.

Organ Fountains, Villa d'Este

All place names, buildings and monuments which have a main entry are printed in heavy type. Map references also appear in heavy type and refer to Central Rome Maps between pages 37–53.

S. Maria in Vallicella [Chiesa Nuo